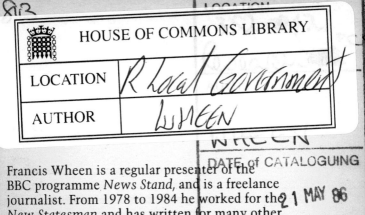
Francis Wheen is a regular presenter of the
BBC programme *News Stand*, and is a freelance
journalist. From 1978 to 1984 he worked for the
New Statesman and has written for many other
papers including the *Times*, the *Guardian*, the
Sunday Times, the *Observer*, the *Daily Mirror*,
the *Los Angeles Times*, *New Socialist*, the
Listener and the *Literary Review*. He edited
World View 1982 published by Pluto Press and
has written two books on contemporary
history: *The Sixties* and *Television* published
by Century.

FRANCIS WHEEN

The Battle
for London

Pluto  Press

LONDON AND SYDNEY

First published in 1985 by Pluto Press Limited, The Works, 105a Torriano
Avenue, London NW5 2RX
and Pluto Press Australia Limited, PO Box 199, Leichhardt,
New South Wales 2040, Australia

Copyright © Francis Wheen, 1985

Text designed by Millions Design
Cover designed by Clive Challis A.Gr.R.

Phototypeset by AKM Associates (UK) Ltd,
Ajmal House, Hayes Road, Southall, London
Printed in Great Britain by Cox & Wyman Limited, Reading

ISBN 0 7453 0054 5

Contents

I should like to thank all the staff at the GLC who were so unfailingly helpful to me, and especially staff of the GLC's wonderful research library. For the government even to consider abolishing such a library is an act of crass philistinism. I am particularly grateful to Stephen Rees at the GLC and Paul Crane at Pluto Press for setting up the project and for arranging such an impressively fast production schedule. Finally, a vote of gratitude to Joan Smith, who helped in every possible way, and several impossible ways as well.

This book is dedicated to the people of London.

1 The modern city

> I am a Tory and have been brought up as one. I
> have been brought up to believe that the
> burden of proof is on the man [*sic*] who
> advocates change. If he does not satisfy that
> burden of proof, change should not be made.
>> *Patrick Jenkin, Secretary of State for the*
>> *Environment, Conservative Party Conference,*
>> *October 1983*

Why does the government want to make London the
only capital city west of the river Elbe without a directly
elected council to speak and act on behalf of its citizens?

Good question. Glad you asked. The only trouble is
that the government hasn't given an answer. It's given
about a dozen answers instead, most of them contradicting one another. At any given moment it's hard to
know which particular answer we are supposed to
believe.

For instance, are the government's abolition proposals
inspired by hostility to the political complexion of the
GLC? Perish the thought, according to the government. A
ministerial briefing note from the Department of the
Environment in February 1984 made this clear:

> The government rejects suggestions that
> abolition is simply a political device to remove
> Labour councils.

Fair enough. But only a month later this was directly
contradicted by a senior member of that same government, Norman Tebbit, who said:

> The Labour Party is the party of division. In its
> present form it represents a threat to the
> democratic values and institutions on which
> our parliamentary system is based. The GLC is
> typical of this new, modern, divisive version of
> socialism. It must be defeated. So we shall
> abolish the GLC.

So! The GLC is being abolished in order to defeat socialism. Patrick Jenkin and his colleagues at the Department of the Environment could be forgiven for feeling pretty annoyed with Tebbit for letting the cat out of the bag quite so spectacularly after they'd spent many months doggedly insisting that party politics had nothing to do with their objections to the GLC.

Tebbit's version certainly has the ring of honesty. The GLC and the Metropolitan County Councils are to be abolished if the government has its way; they are all under Labour control and have therefore come into conflict with the present government. The other county councils are, by and large, controlled by the Conservative Party; there is no suggestion of abolishing *them*. Hardly anyone apart from Patrick Jenkin can seriously believe that this is merely a coincidence.

So what reasons does the government give for abolishing the GLC? You may well ask. Perhaps the GLC is being abolished in order to save money? During 1983 and 1984 Patrick Jenkin and his colleagues persistently claimed that abolition of the GLC would be a boon to ratepayers. As Jenkin said in October 1983:

> It seems to me inevitable that substantial
> savings will be made.

No clue was given as to how 'substantial' those savings might be, since the government hadn't bothered to cost the exercise, but the clear implication was that cost-cutting *was* a reason for abolishing the GLC. During the 1983 general election Margaret Thatcher herself made the connection between abolition and savings:

> I do not consider that the GLC is effective in any way. I do consider that it is an enormous drain on the ratepayer.

It is perhaps irrelevant that her claim was untrue – or at least misleading. What mattered was what the government *believed* to be true, and there's no doubt that ministers were convinced that the GLC was a dreadful, profligate creature, milking the ratepayers for money to be spent on undeserving causes. As Norman Tebbit put it:

> Hand in hand with the assault on the interests of the majority of Londoners has gone the encouragement and funding of every minority cult and creation which the mind can imagine.

'Minority cult' apparently refers to groups such as women, black people and gay people. But no matter. Facts have seldom been allowed to disturb prejudices, as the campaign against the GLC emphatically proves. For instance, in January 1984 Patrick Jenkin claimed:

> Extravagant spending has pushed rates to intolerably high levels.

Where is this extravagant spending? Until 1983, local councils had consistently 'underspent' the government's targets. And in 1983 – 4 the local government 'overspend' of £771 million was only 0.6 per cent of the planned total for public spending. In fact, total spending by local government has fallen in real terms (that is, after allowing for inflation).

Nevertheless, the myths are hard to dislodge. Nigel Lawson, the Chancellor of the Exchequer, announced in January 1984 that

> While central government has been reducing its manpower [*sic*] and looking for savings, local authority current spending in England has been rising.

Not so. Between 1978–9 and 1983–4, current expenditure rose as follows:

○ Central government: +101 per cent
○ Local government: +80 per cent

In other words, local councils' spending was growing much more slowly than that of central government – the government of which Messrs Lawson and Jenkin are members.

But still ministers are adamant that huge savings can somehow be found if the GLC is abolished. Patrick Jenkin told the House of Commons in February 1984 that

> the GLC rate has gone through the roof. There has been a 218 per cent increase in four years.

This is utterly misleading. Over the four years, 1979–80 to 1983–4, the GLC's *gross* precept rose by 110 per cent. In other words, the GLC increased its spending by enough to require a rate increase of 110 per cent over that period. The fact that the GLC's *net* precept – or the rate actually charged – rose by almost twice as much was caused entirely by the government's withdrawal of block grant. If the government wants to blame someone, perhaps it should try blaming itself – and then, no doubt, abolishing itself.

So it seems clear enough: the government claims that it is abolishing the GLC for financial reasons. As one of Jenkin's colleagues at the Department of the Environment, William Waldegrave, told the *Standard* in March 1984:

> I can certainly say that if we have not saved money when the whole process is complete, if we don't show a benefit to London ratepayers, then we shall have failed.

But nothing is that simple in the convoluted logic of the present government. Waldegrave himself, in the same interview, immediately went on to use quite another criterion for 'success':

The real measure of our success will be
whether, in 1988, people are demonstrating in
the streets to demand the restoration of the
GLC.

In any case, Patrick Jenkin himself seems to have had
second thoughts about the wisdom of justifying the
abolition of the GLC on the grounds that it would
produce savings. An independent study of the White
Paper *Streamlining the Cities*, in which the government
put forward its proposals for abolishing the GLC, was
undertaken by the accountants Coopers and Lybrand.
They were not impressed:

Our overall conclusion is that the
government's claims for substantial savings are
not supported by our analysis: indeed we
conclude that there are unlikely to be any net
savings as a result of the structural changes
proposed by the government, and that there
could be significant extra costs.

Jenkin could hardly argue that Coopers and Lybrand
were part of some monstrous left-wing conspiracy, so he
hastily back-tracked instead:

The Coopers report alleges that issues relating
to expenditure are central to the government's
case for abolition. That is not so.

Eh? In that case, why *does* the government want to
abolish the GLC? Jenkin continued:

We are proposing abolition because the GLC
and the Metropolitan County Councils have
too few real functions to justify a separate,
directly elected upper tier of local government
in those areas.

Since then, this has become a familiar line, repeated
almost *ad nauseam* by ministers from the Department of
the Environment. William Waldegrave, for example:

The functions of the GLC have been steadily

disappearing over many years. There is simply not enough left for it to do to justify its continued existence.

The chorus has been joined enthusiastically by Kenneth Baker, the minister who was brought into the department in 1984 with the specific task of countering the GLC's successful publicity campaign. In an interview with Max Hastings of the *Standard* in October 1984, shortly after his appointment, Baker said:

> You ask people in the street what they think the GLC does, and after this vast publicity campaign you find people imagining it runs the telephones or the post office. In reality, it does absurdly little – that's why we're abolishing it. It now controls only one London-wide thing – the Fire Brigade.

Baker obviously liked the sound of this line about the GLC controlling nothing but the Fire Brigade, as he has repeated it many times since. Needless to say, it is pure fantasy. So, for the benefit of the minister – and to put right those 'people in the street' who allegedly think the GLC runs the telephones – it might be worth setting out a list of some of the GLC's real functions.

Planning
The GLC is the planning authority for London and produces the Greater London Development Plan. Other duties include:
○ Preservation of listed buildings
○ Planning authority for Covent Garden
○ Mineral extraction
○ Treatment of derelict land
○ Protection of the Green Belt

Transport
The GLC is in charge of transport planning and co-ordination throughout London. Duties include:

- ○ Control of metropolitan roads (about 900 miles)
- ○ Building, improving and maintaining these roads
- ○ Grants for passenger services (including British Rail)
- ○ Road safety
- ○ Development and maintenance of the urban traffic-control system
- ○ Traffic management on all roads except trunk roads, including traffic-regulation orders (such as the creation of one-way streets and bus lanes), pedestrian crossings, traffic lights, street naming and numbering
- ○ Drafting traffic regulations
- ○ Helping groups with special needs, for example people with disabilities
- ○ Maintenance of Thames bridges
- ○ Maintenance, construction and modernization of Thames piers
- ○ Maintenance and improvement of Thames embankment
- ○ Maintenance and safety observation of Thames tunnels
- ○ Woolwich ferry

Housing

The GLC is responsible for dealing with London-wide housing needs. Duties include:

- ○ Research and information (on housing need, condition of property and so on)
- ○ New building
- ○ Assistance to bodies dealing with homeless people
- ○ Arranging mobility schemes for council tenants wanting to move from one area to another
- ○ Running seaside and country homes for retired council tenants
- ○ Control of Thamesmead
- ○ Home loans

○ Improvements to current and former GLC
   houses and flats

Health and safety
○ Fire service (including fire prevention)
○ Control of building construction in Inner
   London
○ Thames Barrier and other flood defences
○ Refuse disposal for all London
○ Monitoring hazardous chemical waste and
   researching air and noise pollution
○ Emergency planning

Arts and recreation
○ Parks and open spaces (including Hampstead
   Heath, Mile End Park, Blackheath, etc.)
○ Sport facilities (including Crystal Palace and
   numerous playing-fields)
○ Coaching and competitions (including the
   London Marathon), grants to sports bodies
○ Facilities for children (including Thamesday
   festival, Kenwood lakeside concerts, Holland
   Park Open Air Theatre, Horse Shows, etc.)
○ Museums (including Geffrye, Horniman as
   well as financial support for Museum of
   London)
○ Historic houses (Kenwood, Marble Hill House,
   Rangers House)
○ South Bank (the GLC runs the Royal Festival
   Hall and Queen Elizabeth Hall and gives
   money to the National Theatre and National
   Film Theatre)
○ Assistance to other cultural bodies
   (including community arts as well as the
   London Festival Ballet and the English
   National Opera)
○ River Thames and other waterways (including
   eight Thames piers, riverside amenities and
   canal-side parks)
○ Tourism

Industry and employment
- ○ Funding of the Greater London Enterprise Board
- ○ Assistance for employment projects
- ○ Conference and exhibition centres
- ○ Initiating proposals for inner-city regeneration

Policy studies, research and intelligence
- ○ Collection of detailed information on London from many sources, and dissemination in printed form or on to computer
- ○ Policy studies on strategic London issues (policies for elderly people, tourism, etc.)

Services to other bodies and the general public
- ○ Data processing (for London boroughs, Thames Water, House of Lords and – ironically – the Department of the Environment)
- ○ Supplies of goods and materials (customers include London boroughs and other bodies)
- ○ Historic records and history library
- ○ Management of superannuation funds

Judicial services
- ○ Funds magistrates' courts in Outer London
- ○ Provides accommodation for Outer London magistrates' courts
- ○ Funds probation committees in Outer London
- ○ Funds Greater London coroners

Community relations
- ○ Assistance for disabled people, single homeless, one-parent families, children, the elderly
- ○ Grants to voluntary bodies
- ○ Support for ethnic minorities and women (including promotion of equal opportunities and funding of child-care)
- ○ Reviewing law and order in London (including vandalism and racial harassment)

Quite a list. But ministers continue to pretend that the GLC has nothing to do except run the Fire Brigade.

☐ **The government claims that the public backs its attempt to abolish the GLC. But all the evidence suggests otherwise. MORI polls have shown large and growing support for the GLC among Londoners. Hostility to abolition among Londoners has risen from 54 per cent to 66 per cent. A survey conducted for *The London Programme* in October 1984 found 74 per cent opposed to abolition.**

On 7 February 1984 Syd Bidwell MP asked the Prime Minister what representations she had received from Londoners favouring the government's policy of abolishing the GLC. Her reply: 'I have received about 20 such representations.'

As the list of the GLC's duties suggests, London is a vast, complex and diverse city. Before proceeding to examine what the government intends to do to it, it is instructive to recall how the present system for running London evolved. After all, it is unlikely that the GLC would have acquired so many functions and duties over the years unless it had been meeting a real need. How did this need arise?

A voice for London

London may be an ancient city, but it had a long wait before it was granted the right to some form of local self-government. It was not until 1855 that parliament set up the Metropolitan Board of Works, responsible for 'the better management of the metropolis in respect of sewerage, drainage, paving, cleansing, lighting and improvements'.

The board had some success in improving public health and it certainly proved the need for a unified all-London administration. But it also had serious shortcomings. One was a simple lack of powers. Another was a lack of democracy: the board was not elected by the people it was supposed to serve. Members were appointed from indirectly elected local boards and from bodies such as the City Corporation.

In 1867 a select committee recommended that the board should be directly elected and should thus become the Municipal Council of London. The council would take over gas and water supply, railway planning and other matters of public interest. However, nothing was done about this proposal because the City Corporation and other vested interests lobbied against it.

For the next 20 years the City Corporation continued to block every attempt to reform London's government. But a parliamentary inquiry in 1887 found that the methods used by the City in its campaigns included bribery, the founding of bogus organizations, false reports and violent behaviour.

With the opposition to reform thus discredited – and with the Metropolitan Board of Works itself being accused of corruption – parliament was at last obliged to create a new County of London, to be governed by a directly elected council. In 1889 the London County Council (LCC) was established, starting the tradition of the directly elected administration for London which has continued uninterrupted ever since – but which will now end in 1986 if the present government has its way, thus putting the clock back by 100 years.

☐ **The present attempt to abolish the GLC is by no means the first. Indeed, there is a sense of *déjà vu* about the whole business. As long ago as 1898 the Conservative government of Lord Salisbury proposed breaking up the LCC and transferring its powers and duties to the boroughs – a process known as 'Tenification', because Salisbury intended that ten municipalities should take over from the**

17

LCC. A booklet put out in February 1898 by the Progressive Party (an alliance of Liberals, Radicals and Socialists, whose members included Sidney Webb) contains many comments which have a familiar ring to them: 'The only effect [of Tenification] would be an increase of rates in each district. The Moderates, who knew everything about it, admitted that very few powers can be transferred. Mr Whitmore, for instance, says: "I believe all those who know anything about local government in London perfectly understand that it is impossible and impracticable to make any large amount of transfer of powers from the County Council to the local authorities." ' Under the London Government Act 1899 some powers were transferred to the newly created metropolitan boroughs, but the LCC still retained enough to make it a powerful municipal force.

In the first half of this century the LCC went from strength to strength. In 1903 it started electrification of London's trams and introduced a low fares policy. In the following year it became the education authority for London: its work in this area laid the foundations for many of the provisions of the famous 1944 Education Act, and its plan for 'multi-schools' foreshadowed comprehensive education.

In 1930 the LCC took over health and Poor Law work in London. The high standards the LCC set in health and housing looked forward to the creation of the National Health Service and the post-war reconstruction. The stature of local government was also enhanced by the involvement of nationally famous politicians such as Herbert Morrison, a member of the LCC from 1922 to 1945 and leader from 1934 to 1940. It was Morrison who opened the new Waterloo Bridge in 1945 – a bridge that had been built by the LCC in defiance of central government, and therefore came to symbolize the idea that elected councillors at the LCC might have a better idea of London's needs than the MPs across the river.

> 66 There is no London stock, no standard London speech – there is no common London type. Our origins and our characteristics are very mixed . . . So I'm not sure what London is. I am not sure who the Londoners are. But I love London; I love the Londoners. 99
> Herbert Morrison, 1935

As the geographical area of London expanded and the demands on local government increased, it became obvious that there would have to be changes. It was equally obvious that no upheavals should be contemplated until there had been a full inquiry. So in 1957 the government set up a Royal Commission on Local Government in London, chaired by Sir Edwin Herbert. It was the most thorough review of London's government ever undertaken. When the Herbert Commission reported in 1960, it was unanimous in recommending a two-tier system of government for London, consisting of a Greater London Council and 52 boroughs.

London has changed a good deal in the quarter century since Herbert's inquiry, of course. Nevertheless, much of the report is still applicable today. Moreover, since the present government has refused to conduct any kind of proper inquiry before rushing ahead with its plans for abolishing the GLC, it is worth remembering what was said when there *was* a royal commission on London's government:

Local government, as we see it, is not just a machine or a piece of organization . . . Local government seems to us to be much more like a living thing, an organism, in which each part

19

or function is not self-contained or connected externally with other parts. Each part is integrally concerned with each other part . . . While, therefore, the actual work and thought and feeling of professional administrators, elected members and electors has of necessity to be separately described, one has to remember that they do not function in separation but that each is dependent on and influences the others . . . Local government is with us an instance of democracy at work, and no amount of potential administrative efficiency could make up for the loss of active participation in the work by capable, public-spirited people elected by, responsible to, and in touch with those who elect them.

Herbert went on to consider some alternative options which had been suggested for London's government. Some of these are the very same suggestions that have been revived by the present government. One, for instance, was a surrender of important powers to central government. Herbert argued that this would be 'the death knell of local government' in London and would cause endless administrative confusion.

Another suggestion rejected by Herbert which has also been revived by the present government as a way of replacing the GLC is the idea of transferring some of the council's duties to *ad hoc* bodies – quangos, joint boards and committees, and so on. Herbert was contemptuous of the proposal: these bodies would either be 'the creatures of central government' or would be 'responsible to no one'. In either case, they would not represent the people of London. But the Herbert Report had another reason for disapproving of the proposal:

The second objection is that, as we have shown, so many of London's problems are interlinked. What is needed is some means of considering them as a whole and dealing with them. It is no solution to separate them still further by giving each to some specially designed *ad hoc* body.

Herbert's recommendations were largely accepted by the government, and in 1963 the London Government Act created a new administrative system for the capital, consisting of:

- ○ the Greater London Council, formed from the London County Council, Middlesex County Council and parts of Hertfordshire, Essex, Kent and Surrey;
- ○ the Inner London Education Authority, responsible for education in the 13 inner boroughs;
- ○ a second tier of local councils below the GLC, made up of 32 borough councils and the City of London (an anachronism which seems to go on for ever).

This is the structure that still exists today.

❝ The sum of local needs and wishes does not add up to the total view of the region and it is because they do not that there is a need for a strategic authority in the first place. ❞
Sir James Swaffield, Director-General of the GLC, 1977

After the Conservatives won control of the GLC in 1977 they appointed Sir Frank Marshall (now Lord Marshall and Deputy Chairman of the Conservative Party) to conduct an inquiry into London's government. It was expected that the report might be unsympathetic to the GLC. In fact, however, the Marshall Report found that the council performed an essential job; the report even recommended an extension of the GLC's powers. As Marshall argued:

I have taken the view from the start that the existence of a metropolitan authority is necessary to enable London government to function properly. The total interest of London as a whole transcends that of its constituent parts, their local needs and individual aspirations. It must be cared for by a corporate body charged with taking an overall view of issues and events in metropolitan terms.

It seemed that the GLC's future was assured.

> 66 Now a great place like this really can't afford to be left to the arguments and petty quarrels of 32 different London boroughs, so there must be some guiding hand which looks at the future of London and the quality of life of the people who live here. 99
>
> Sir Frank Marshall, *The London Programme*, 3 May 1981

Let battle commence

The Conservative government led by Margaret Thatcher came into conflict with local councils almost as soon as it was elected in May 1979. This was inevitable. Thatcher and her colleagues had made it clear that they intended to 'put the squeeze' on local authorities; a number of local authorities had made it equally clear that they felt they'd been squeezed enough already.

Since then, matters have gone from bad to worse. Local government experts of all political hues find it hard to remember a time when relations between Whitehall and the town halls have been as appalling as they are today – indeed, it would not be much of an exaggeration to say that central and local government are not even on speaking terms anymore.

This is because some local councils saw it as their duty to try to alleviate the effects of central government policies in their areas. They believed that at a time of recession and high unemployment, local services were needed more than ever – yet the government told them that they had to cut their spending. They refused, and because local councils still had a fair measure of autonomy from central government, they were able to get away with it.

But not for long. The government reacted by arming itself with more and more controls over local councils, including tough penalties for 'overspenders'. Several councils had their grant from the government removed altogether, leaving them entirely dependent on the rates.

The setting of a rate was just about the last bit of autonomy left to local councils – and the government's next action was to stop even that. In 1980, Tom King, then Minister for Local Government, had said:

> We have specifically left local authorities
> freedom to fix their own rates . . . We've made
> our contribution. It's then up to local
> authorities – without any power for us to
> intervene – to determine what they actually do
> and how they fix their rate levies. If we'd
> started to determine their rate levies for them,
> then I'd accept that that would be a major
> threat to local democracy.

By 1984 this 'major threat to local democracy' had become part of the government's policy. 'Rate-capping' allowed the Secretary of State for the Environment, Patrick Jenkin, to tell a local council how big a rate it could levy – and if it disobeyed, he could send commissioners in to take over the running of the council. This was the same Patrick Jenkin who had said in 1973:

> I would very much rather see local authorities
> have a fair degree of discretion and be prepared
> to take on their shoulders the full
> responsibility for their decisions, rather than
> that they should become simply glorified
> agents for Whitehall.

By 1984 Jenkin apparently felt differently. It might seem laughable that a minister such as Jenkin should imagine that he has a better understanding of the needs of a particular locality – Leicester, say, or Swindon – than the elected councillors in that area, but to the councils on the receiving end of Jenkin's diktats it was no joke. In December 1984 Jenkin announced statutory rate limits for 18 councils on his 'hit list' which would force them to cut their rates the following April by up to 56 per cent.

While turning the screw on local councils over the past six years, the government has had a nagging problem. Margaret Thatcher came to power having promised to abolish rates altogether within the lifetime of a parliament. Rates were reckoned to be an unpopular tax, and Thatcher believed that by ending them she would win many extra votes.

However, there was one unanswered question: what should be put in their place? Local councils had to raise money *somehow*. Would a local sales tax or a poll tax be any fairer than the rates? The Prime Minister set up a cabinet committee, chaired by William Whitelaw, to look into the matter.

In January 1983 Whitelaw's committee told the Prime Minister that there was no alternative to the rates, given that she was not prepared even to consider the idea of a local income tax (she thinks this proposal would be even less popular than rates).

This left her in an awkward position. She wanted to call a general election within a few months and she felt that she must have some sort of radical reform in local government to put into the manifesto. If she couldn't promise to abolish rates, she must find some other way of showing that she intended to 'get to grips' with local government.

Whitelaw's cabinet committee had a ready-made solution for her: abolish the GLC and the six Metropolitan Counties. These councils, all Labour-controlled, were the biggest and therefore the most visible of the local authorities which had been attempting to stop their areas being laid waste by the policies of central government. Sure enough, abolition of the GLC and the Metropolitan Counties was hastily inserted in the Conservatives' manifesto.

Recently, the government has claimed that the pledge came only after a long and thorough consideration of the issue. For instance, in December 1984 Patrick Jenkin told the House of Commons: 'I took part in the year-long discussions before the election which led to this commitment.' You might think that at some stage the leader of the Conservative Group on the GLC, Alan Greengross, would have been brought into those discussions. But he wasn't. He didn't even know that such discussions were taking place. The first he heard of any Tory commitment to abolish the GLC was *three days* before it was made public in the party's election manifesto on 18 May 1983.

☐ **In October 1984 Nigel Spearing MP asked the Prime Minister if she would give the date at which she became publicly committed to the policy of abolishing the GLC. She replied: 'On 18 May 1983.' In other words, nine days *after* the announcement of the date of the 1983 general election.**

The belief that the promise to abolish the GLC was made on the spur of the moment is shared by many Conservatives. Rodney Gent, a Tory member of the GLC, says that the insertion of the pledge in the manifesto, 'surrounded as it was by a factually incorrect statement of the powers of local authorities, bears all the hallmarks of a late decision. The powers of the GLC cannot be returned to the London boroughs [as the manifesto had claimed] because the boroughs never had them in the first place.'

The unhappiness of Tory backbenchers in parliament is just as great as that of their colleagues at the GLC, and was summed up by Hugh Dykes MP during the Second Reading debate on GLC abolition in December 1984:

Although many keep quiet, it is widely known that this rather crude and unconsidered Bill was originally born from an abrupt and primitive political decision arising out of the worst kind of sudden-whim, sudden-hunch politics ... The whole measure rests on no outside, independent, searching expert inquiry as has always been the case in our United Kingdom tradition ... I am sad that our cabinet colleagues at no time insisted upon a proper examination of this hugely complex matter before the die was cast in the creation of a thoroughly bad, ruthless Bill which has left the civil service smarting and furious and the Conservative Party divided and miserable as never before.

From the moment when the promise to abolish the GLC popped up in the Tory manifesto in May 1983, the government has consistently and obstinately refused to hold any kind of inquiry into the plan. Having dreamed up the idea on the spur of the moment, ministers have been understandably reluctant to have it subjected to rigorous scrutiny.

The Herbert Commission, which preceded the creation of the GLC in 1963, sat for three years and took millions of words of evidence. Today, however, the government seems to believe that it must move at breakneck speed. Here is a timetable of the idea of abolishing the GLC, from the moment when it was no more than a glint in its parents' eyes to the moment when – ministers hope – it will become a reality.

○ **May 1983**: Conservatives, with no prior warning, promise to abolish GLC if elected.
○ **October 1983**: government publishes half-baked White Paper titled, absurdly, *Streamlining the Cities*. Response is almost unanimously hostile. Government retires to lick its wounds.

- **January 1984**: end of 'consultation period' for White Paper. Thousands of organizations and individuals have sent responses, but government refuses to publish these or to say how many were in favour of abolition.
- **March 1984**: government publishes 'Paving Bill' intended to abolish 1985 GLC elections and install a Conservative administration at County Hall in May 1985 for the last year of the GLC's life.
- **June-July 1984**: House of Lords wrecks Paving Bill. Amendment supporting elections in 1985 and criticizing the installation of an unelected council is carried by 48 votes. Government is forced to delete large chunks of Bill and allow existing councillors to continue in office until 1986
- **July 1984**: government publishes what it describes as a 'Yellow Document', supposed to be a response to all the representations received on its White Paper. But in fact proposals from *Streamlining the Cities* survive virtually unchanged.
- **July-November 1984**: government fails to use its powers under Section 5 of Paving Act to request information from GLC. Of the five requests received before publication of the main Abolition Bill only one came from a government department, even though Section 5 had been specifically introduced 'for the purpose of facilitating the formulation and . . . implementation of proposals' to abolish the GLC.
- **November 1984**: government publishes Local Government Bill which is meant to bring about abolition of GLC. Proposals still as muddled and anti-democratic as ever.
- **December 1984**: Second Reading debate on Abolition bill. Ted Heath and other senior Conservative backbenchers make hostile

speeches. Government majority reduced to 23 on one amendment. *Daily Telegraph* reports: 'The government's chances of getting its Bill to abolish the GLC and the six Metropolitan Counties on to the statute book intact appeared in serious doubt yesterday.'

○ **April 1986**: GLC abolished – if the government has its way.

Why the rush? Patrick Jenkin says that it's because he has to get all the relevant legislation through parliament in time to abolish the GLC on April Fools' Day in 1986. But where did this deadline of April 1986 come from? From the head of Patrick Jenkin. There is nothing particularly sacrosanct about the date, but Jenkin is convinced that there is, and that legislation must be rushed through. Hence his vagueness about how much money will be saved by the abolition of the GLC and about how the system will work if the GLC goes: he is making it up as he goes along. As one Tory backbencher, Anthony Beaumont-Dark, said during the debate on the Paving Bill: 'The Bill, if I may say so, was virtually drafted on the back of an envelope, because it seemed a good idea at the time.'

□ **Kenneth Baker, the new Minister for Local Government, claimed on Radio 4's *Today* programme in September 1984 that 'I believe and have always believed in the abolition of the GLC consistently since I represented London back in the 1960s.' The Minister obviously has problems with his memory. In a parliamentary debate in March 1971 he spoke of the GLC in very different terms, saying 'it has progressive and expanding programmes, it is making life better for Londoners, and it will make it infinitely better for Londoners in the 1970s and the 1980s.' Moreover, in 1977 Kenneth Baker**

co-wrote a pamphlet called *Maybe It's Because We're Londoners* in which he argued that 'the strategic role of the GLC should be enhanced.'

Since the government's proposals were cobbled together without any thought, it is perhaps hardly surprising that they have come under fire from almost every individual and organization with any interest or expertise in the subject. Nor is it surprising that the government refused to publish the reactions it received to *Streamlining the Cities* or to say whether any of them supported the White Paper.

Nevertheless, the sheer scale of unanimity in opposition to the government's plans is still unprecedented. It is worth reproducing a few of the thousands of comments which have been made in the past 18 months, to give a flavour of the strength of feeling:

Cardinal Hume, Archbishop of Westminster:
> The existence of a central elected body has enabled services to be provided for a variety of groups whose needs could be neglected by individual boroughs.

Financial Times, 12 December 1984:
> There are certain criteria which must be fulfilled for changes to be acceptable. The first is that the new arrangements stand a reasonable chance of being an improvement on the old. The second is that accountability is not reduced, so that pressure for efficiency and sensitivity to local aspirations is not diminished. The third is that democracy and democratic principles are not violated. The Bill fails on all three counts.

GLC Conservative Group, January 1984:
> The structure that is proposed, where indeed any real structure can actually be identified,

29

would inevitably lead to a proliferation of commissions, quangos, boards, bodies and committees. Such a fragmented arrangement would be more complex, more confusing to the public, more bureaucratic and actually more costly than a relatively simple structure, for all its faults, that it seeks to streamline.

Royal Town Planning Institute:
> The present proposals appear to have been hastily put together ... The institute is totally opposed to the abolition of the GLC ... The proposed replacement structure is totally inadequate to deal with the very real metropolitan-wide problems.

London Chamber of Commerce and Industry:
> This is a prescription for additional costs, delay and confusion.

Times, 24 November 1984:
> The abolition Bill can be examined in vain for any expression of a general philosophy of the role of government in society ... It is a document lacking any sense of future ... It is a document lacking coherent principles for local administration.

Guardian, 23 November 1984:
> It is impossible to read yesterday's Local Government Bill – which abolishes the GLC and its regional counterparts – without asking one question: What on earth is the point of it all?

Any play which received notices like that would probably be taken off forthwith; but the government's much abused show somehow carries on regardless.

The GLC and the Metropolitan Counties have commissioned a number of outside experts to look at particular aspects of the government's plans. (The government itself has commissioned no expert studies at all – presumably because it knows that its proposals would instantly crumble.) All these independent studies have found serious flaws in the proposals for abolishing the GLC.

Leading accountants Coopers and Lybrand concluded that there were 'unlikely to be any net savings' as a result of abolition of the Metropolitan Counties and 'there could be significant extra costs.'

Another firm, PA Management Consultants, looked into the non-financial aspects of abolition and concluded:

> The new structure will be more complex than
> the existing one ... Overall, we have been
> unable to find a single service where the
> quality of service to the local elector is likely
> to be improved as a result of the change in
> structure. In many cases we believe that there
> will be a marked decline in quality.

Research by academics has come to similar conclusions. The Greater London Group at the London School of Economics commented:

> We are forced to conclude from the rejection
> by the government of ordinary and established
> democratic processes, and by the emptiness of
> the White Paper, that the abolition of the GLC
> and the Metropolitan County Councils was
> decided on primarily because of the need to
> include something in the party manifesto
> which would capitalize on the belief that local
> authorities were unpopular with part of the
> electorate.

Since many of the GLC's functions will be passed to 'joint boards' (in other words, quangos) or 'joint committees' of councillors from different boroughs, the Institute of Local Government Studies at Birmingham University produced a report called *Joint Boards and Joint*

Committees: An Evaluation, based on research covering more than 60 examples of joint action between local authorities.

All previous inquiries had found that joint boards and committees were an unsuccessful idea. The Herbert Commission, for instance, said:

> It is inconceivable to us that bodies of this kind could contribute much to a solution of the major problems we have in mind.

The study by the Institute of Local Government Studies confirmed this belief. It found:

> The presumption in the White Paper as to the effectiveness of joint action with regard to accountability or performance is not borne out by the historical evidence. Joint boards and committees have been widely viewed as being in conflict with the principles of local democracy.

The report added that the joint boards and committees would make inefficient use of resources, would inevitably be drawn into conflicts between boroughs, would be slow to decide anything and would be hideously complex. It concluded:

> It seems inconceivable to us that the new arrangements will produce a system which is more comprehensible and accessible to individual citizens. A two-tiered local government certainly has its problems but a system consisting of a host of separate joint boards and joint committees of dubious accountability, backed up by a new range of central government controls, all superimposed upon the existing district tier, seems to us considerably more confused and problematical.

The government gets angry at criticisms like that, since it denies that there are going to be joint boards taking over GLC functions. Time and again it has tried to convince the public that the GLC's job will simply be taken over by the individual boroughs. As Patrick Jenkin said in July 1984:

> Contrary to the impression given by recent misleading advertising, almost all the functions will devolve either individually or jointly on to the local democratically elected councils . . . Abolition will therefore mean the decentralization of powers to the local level.

It sounds delightful – who could possibly object to services becoming 'more accessible and more responsive', as Patrick Jenkin claims?

Unfortunately, it isn't true. The government says that 75 per cent of the GLC's expenditure is going straight to the London boroughs 'and the balance, which is the Fire Board, will actually be controlled by the borough councillors.'

But the figure of 75 per cent can be obtained only by ignoring certain things. It ignores, for instance, the cost of servicing the GLC's debts (which are to be managed by a quango called the Residuary Body). The figure also leaves out the cost of housing deficits and the GLC's subsidy to London Regional Transport. On the other hand, services for which borough councils will have little discretion – for which, in fact, they will do little more than write the cheque – *are* added in as part of the 75 per cent. These include London-wide grants and concessionary fares.

Once the government's misleading figures are un-scrambled and the sums are done correctly, a rather different picture begins to emerge. Only 15.7 per cent of the spending of the GLC and ILEA in 1984–5 will be transferred to the boroughs' control. The rest will go to quangos or joint boards or Whitehall. Taking just GLC spending alone, 30.9 per cent will go to the boroughs.

Moreover, those items of spending which will be left to the discretion of borough councils are precisely the ones which the boroughs are least likely to fund – the GLC's initiatives in industry and employment, support for ethnic minorities, women's rights and gay rights. Some borough councils will refuse to pay for these because they have political objections. But even those boroughs which think that jobs, women and so on are important will find it hard to raise the money, since those boroughs will probably already be under pressure from rate-capping.

> **❝Our boroughs will not be able to cope with the government's proposed transfer of powers from the GLC. Administrative chaos will hit London in 1986. With many of us facing the prospect of rate-capping the government must realize that they cannot keep heaping responsibilities on to local councils while simultaneously withdrawing essential money.❞**
> Margaret Hodge, Chair of Association of London
> Authorities

The government's claim that '75 per cent' of the GLC's spending will be 'devolved' to boroughs is thus utter hogwash. According to calculations done by the GLC finance department – figures which the government has been unable to refute – almost *half* the GLC's spending will be taken over by quangos, joint boards, trusts and so on. Another 19 per cent will be controlled by Whitehall, which hardly justifies the government's trumpetings about making local government more local.

It is also untrue to say that the Fire Board will be the only quango created as a consequence of the GLC's abolition. Between eight and 15 quangos or joint boards will take over current GLC functions. Some of these will be quangos that already exist, which will have their powers and duties extended; others will be quangos specially created for the occasion. One cannot be more precise about their number because the government's plans for how the system will work are themselves in such a shambles that not even Whitehall knows how many quangos will be necessary. However, one can be reasonably definite about the following ones:

○ **Fire Joint Board**. Will administer the London Fire Brigade (with four 'area boards' beneath the London-wide board) as well as taking responsibility for civil defence and petroleum licensing.

○ **Historic Buildings and Monuments Commission**. This quango already exists. It will have to take over the GLC's duties in connection with Historic Buildings.

○ **Thames Water Authority**. This quango has existed since the *last* chaotic reorganization of local government, when responsibility for sewage was taken away from councils and given to unelected water boards. Now it will take over the GLC's responsibility for land drainage and the Thames Barrier.

○ **Residuary Body**. Will deal with the GLC's external debt, superannuation, compensation payments, property and computing.

○ **Statutory Body.** Will deal with collective grant-making powers of the London boroughs.

○ **Supplies Quango**. To be established by boroughs to take over the GLC's job of central buying of supplies, which gives economies of scale.

○ **London Regional Transport**. Already exists: in 1984 this unaccountable quango took over London Transport from the GLC.

○ **Waste Disposal Joint Board**. Will have to be established if, as seems likely, the boroughs cannot work out a 'voluntary scheme of co-operation'.

○ **London Planning Commission**. Will

advise the Secretary of State for the
Environment on London-wide planning issues.

Past experience shows that when local government
services are put in the hands of quangos, the services
become less efficient. Both sewers and ambulances used
to be controlled by local authorities; since they were
given to quangos they have become far more costly to
administer and more remote from the people they are
meant to serve.

It seems certain that the same will happen this time.
Consider, for instance, the proposed London Planning
Commission. There is no argument about the fact that
planning is essential: it determines how land is used,
how the environment is protected and improved and
how amenities, transport and other services are provided
in a co-ordinated way. Without planning, London would
be in a state of chaos.

At the moment, London-wide planning is the
responsibility of the GLC. After abolition, however, all
strategic decisions connected with London's planning
would be taken in Whitehall. When critics point out
that this looks suspiciously like centralization, rather
than 'devolution' of power, the government replies that it
will be advised by the London Planning Commission,
which will represent the views of London.

Since the Planning Commission will not be elected,
it is difficult to see how it will represent anybody but
itself. However, the government has pointed to a body
called the London and South-East Planning Conference
(more conveniently known as Serplan) as an example of
what can be achieved by planning quangos. Serplan is a
body which brings together representatives of the GLC,
London boroughs and the county and district councils
for Bedfordshire, Berkshire, Buckinghamshire, East
Sussex, Essex, Hampshire, Hertfordshire, the Isle of
Wight, Kent, Oxfordshire, Surrey and West Sussex.
Serplan has only a very small staff and relies heavily on
the GLC for its research and intelligence functions.

Ministers have been fulsome in their praise for

Serplan. But Serplan has not returned the compliment. In November 1984 the government was highly embarrassed when the press obtained copies of a letter which had been sent privately by Serplan to the Department of the Environment. Serplan deplored the plans for abolition of the GLC, which would

> make the Secretary of State the strategic planning authority for Greater London, but without the obligation to prepare an overall and detailed scrutiny through an examination in public.

Serplan also pointed out that the government has refused even to look at the GLC's proposed alterations to the Greater London Development Plan, on the grounds that they are irrelevant because the GLC is to be abolished anyway. But even if the GLC is killed off, London's need for rational planning will not go away. Serplan expressed its concern

> that the government should appear to prefer time, effort and energy to be devoted to resolving the organizational problems which its own proposals are creating rather than to the real problems of London which the GLC has sought to identify and address in its Greater London Development Plan amendments.

The Planning Commission, like the other quangos taking over duties from the GLC, seems certain to take little or no notice of what Londoners actually want. This has already happened at the quangos which are already in operation – the London Regional Transport Board and the London Docklands Development Corporation – where the worst fears of the critics have been confirmed.

The central justification for the government's plan to abolish the GLC thus turns out to be bogus. Patrick Jenkin says that abolition will end 'an expensive and unnecessary two-tier system of local government'. But it won't. Outside London and the other six big cities, the two-tier system of county and district councils will continue exactly as before. If the two-tier system is 'expensive and unnecessary' why are these councils not being abolished as well?

More importantly, however, the government is *not* abolishing an 'unnecessary' tier of local government. This is accepted by almost everyone who has studied the government's proposals, including many people who have no particular reason to support the present ruling group at the GLC. Can it really be the case that Patrick Jenkin is right and everybody else is wrong?

> The streamlining envisaged in the White Paper, whatever might be emotively claimed, does not eliminate a tier of local government. It merely rearranges that tier.
> GLC Conservative Group, January 1984

> The councils are not being abolished; only the councillors will be abolished. All the functions will remain, with no reorganization of the Metropolitan Districts and London boroughs to enable them to become multi-service unitary authorities in their own right. So seven democratically elected, directly accountable councils [GLC and Metropolitan Counties] would be replaced by a mixture of joint committees and joint boards with powers to rate but neither directly elected nor directly accountable.
> *Financial Times*, 8 March 1984

> The government claims duplication will be avoided and a whole layer of local government will be removed and not replaced ... The only 'layer' removed is the cherished right of Londoners and others to elect their own governing body in common with most other large cities in Europe.
> *Guardian*, 23 November 1984

2 On the move

The real benefits of the transport system can only be obtained by using the full range of facilities in a co-ordinated way. There is a tremendous job of work to be done in this area by County Hall.

From a 1977 pamphlet by Kenneth Baker MP, now the minister in charge of GLC abolition

There are many ways of 'getting about' in London – buses, tubes, trains, cars, bicycles, ferries and, of course, Shanks's pony. All of them affect one another. For instance, consider what would happen if more people suddenly started using cars in London. Not only would it greatly increase the hazards to pedestrians and cyclists; it would also mean that fewer people were using public transport. This, in turn, could mean that fares on the buses and tubes would go up while services would be reduced. Consequently, even more people would use cars, causing yet more snarl-ups and accidents.

Meanwhile, what would happen to those people who couldn't afford cars – particularly women, pensioners, ethnic minorities, the handicapped and the unemployed? Quite simply, they would be marooned.

But this is not some kind of hypothetical prediction of what might happen in the future. It is what *has* happened in London for many years, and we have all experienced its effects: waiting on an underground platform for the train that never seems to come; being stuck on a bus in a traffic jam that hasn't moved for quarter of an hour; trying to sleep while juggernauts thunder past outside all night long.

Almost everyone who has stopped to think about it agrees that there is only one solution to the problem: a city as big and complex as London must have a central, elected body which can consider all the different types of transport in the capital and can then organize a system which allows them to work together harmoniously – and allows Londoners to get from A to B as easily as possible.

It was for this reason that in the 1960s the GLC was given responsibility for London Transport as well as for traffic management and highway planning. The point was particularly well made by one MP during the parliamentary debate on the Transport (London) Bill in 1968:

> The purpose of the Bill is to achieve a new concept in transport planning so that all aspects of transport – cars, buses, railways and parking – can be related to each other and to the disposition of office blocks, factories, shops, houses and the routes taken by people to work. This obviously has to be closely co-ordinated with land use.

The speaker was a Conservative called Margaret Thatcher. Since then the need for an 'integrated' transport system like the one she described has not disappeared. But her support for it apparently has, since she is now determined to abolish the one body which can take a 'London-wide' view of transport.

More recently, in 1977, another Conservative MP was one of the authors of a booklet called *Maybe It's Because We're Londoners* which again argued for all aspects of transport to be related to each other:

> The real benefit of the transport system can only be obtained by using the full range of facilities in a co-ordinated way. There is a tremendous job of work to be done in this area by County Hall.

40

There certainly was. And Kenneth Baker MP, the man who wrote those words, made some specific suggestions which the GLC has taken up:

Baker's plan	GLC action
'Public transport carries people more cheaply, with less demand on space and energy, and less environmental damage than private cars. The key to a successful transport policy in London is improved public transport.'	Bus and tube services have been increased and fares reduced to attract more people to public transport. Bus and train routes have been extended to places which didn't have them before. Bus and tube stations have been refurbished.
'A simplified basic fares structure should be introduced, and more flexible schemes are needed to appeal to regular commuters (through rail–bus tickets are a must), special parties and off-peak travellers.'	In 1981 new, simplified 'zonal' fares were created. In 1983 the Travelcard was introduced, valid for buses and tubes.
'Help must continue for the especially vulnerable categories of users such as the elderly and the disabled.'	Free travel on London Transport for the elderly and disabled has been extended; many other services for the disabled have been started, including 'dial-a-ride' and cheap taxi fares.

So is Kenneth Baker pleased to see his plans being put into practice? Unfortunately not: he is now the local government minister with special responsibility for abolishing the GLC. In 1977 he thought the GLC had a 'tremendous job of work' to do; today he claims that it has 'absurdly little' to do.

Yet nobody – not even Kenneth Baker – can seriously deny that London's roads are hopelessly congested for much of the time. You only have to turn on the radio in the morning to hear the familiar litany of traffic jams. There are two possible ways of dealing with the problem.

The first would be to **build more roads and motorways in London, and widen existing roads**. This involves demolishing thousands of homes and gardens – at a time when there is already a shortage of housing – and destroying open spaces. And there's no guarantee that this policy would even achieve its purpose. Research shows that – in a variation on Parkinson's Law – the amount of traffic tends to expand to fill the space available. In other words, if you build more roads in London you will probably get more cars and lorries coming into London. The early-morning radio programmes will still recite the list of traffic jams and hold-ups; it will simply be rather a longer list than it was before.

The alternative approach would be to **accept that London has only a limited amount of space for movement and that this space is used most efficiently by public transport**. A car driving into London in the morning rush hour may well have only one person in it. A bus travelling into town at the same time will contain dozens of passengers, yet will not take up much more road-space than the car.

☐ **Buses are exceptionally efficient users of London's limited road space. Fewer than 2 per cent of vehicles entering central London during the rush hour are buses, but they carry 30 per cent of the people going by road.**

And tube trains – one need hardly point out – use no road-space at all. All that remains to be done is to encourage more people to use public transport.

42

Incredible though it may seem, the government appears to think that the first option is the most sensible solution to the problems of transport in London. In October 1984 Nicholas Ridley, the Transport Secretary, said:

> There is no longer any justification for special taxpayers' support for current expenditure on local transport, for day-to-day expenditure on local needs or for general public transport subsidies.

In other words, public transport is so unimportant to the life of the city that it isn't worth subsidizing. If there were no subsidies for buses and trains, fares would shoot up to ridiculous levels and hardly anyone would use the service. Those who could afford to do so would use cars instead; those who couldn't afford cars would be stranded.

☐ **Outside Britain, almost all major cities recognize that public transport needs proper subsidies if it is to be effective. London Transport's subsidy of 37 per cent is pitiful compared with that of other big cities:**

New York – 72 per cent
Milan – 71 per cent
Brussels – 70 per cent
Berlin – 61 per cent
Paris – 56 per cent

If the government's targets are met, the 37 per cent subsidy for public transport in London will be halved.

The GLC prefers the second option. And so do most Londoners, to judge by opinion polls and by the fact that they do switch to public transport when it is made more attractive. This was proved in 1981 when the GLC introduced its 'Fares Fair' policy – a 32 per cent reduction in ticket prices. After only three months the Law Lords declared the policy illegal. Nevertheless, during the brief period of 'Fares Fair' there was a dramatic change in Londoners' travelling habits:

○ There was a 10 per cent increase in the use of public transport.
○ The number of people entering central London by car during the rush hour fell by 6 per cent.

As a result of the Law Lords' decision, fares on London Transport were doubled. The consequences were predictable: a slump in the use of public transport, a huge increase in the number of cars coming into central London and a rise in the number of road accidents. (One independent study estimated that 6,000 extra people were killed or injured on the roads because of the fare increases.)

In May 1983 – this time without the obstruction of the Law Lords – the GLC reduced fares again, by 13 per cent on the buses and 24 per cent on the underground. It also introduced the Travelcard, which could be used for journeys on both buses and tube trains. Once again, the effects were striking:

○ Passenger traffic on the buses rose by 11 per cent.
○ Passenger traffic on the underground rose by 24 per cent.
○ There were 3,000 fewer casualties on the roads.
○ Sales of Travelcards reached 600,000 by the end of 1983.
○ The number of cars coming into London fell by 10 per cent.

In addition to the fare reduction, the GLC has taken other measures to encourage the use of public transport.

These include:

○ A £60 million programme of modernizing and refurbishing underground stations.

○ The creation of 200 bus lanes, which reduce the likelihood of buses 'bunching' because of traffic jams.

○ Making it easier to transfer from a British Rail train to a tube and vice versa. For instance, new platforms on the British Rail line at West Ham have been linked directly to the London Transport station.

○ A plan to extend the Travelcard to British Rail services.

○ Providing 2,500 car parking spaces at stations in Outer London and beyond.

○ Introducing a more modern design of train on the underground.

○ Installing electronic indicators on underground platforms to show when the next train is due.

○ Starting work on a light railway for Docklands, linking the Isle of Dogs to Tower Hill and Stratford, which is due to open in 1987.

But the government was unimpressed. In 1984 it removed London Transport from the GLC's control and replaced it by a new London Regional Transport Board, answerable only to the Secretary of State. Since then, Londoners have had no say in their public transport system.

London Regional Transport (LRT) is a prototype of the kind of boards which will take over responsibility for many of London's services if the GLC is abolished, so its record during its few months of existence so far is an indication of what we can expect in other areas. And that record is not encouraging.

❝❝London Transport produced its biggest profit in 20 years, the result of carrying more passengers on better

services at relatively lower fares. Do we hear the faintest promise from Mr Ridley that when he takes charge he can match that record or improve on it? We do not. No wonder people are worried. 〝 〞

Standard, 27 March 1984

The first change is that decisions about public transport are now taken in total secrecy. Information which was previously available to the public can no longer be obtained from LRT, even by MPs. This includes statistics for bus and tube mileage, and figures for LRT's financial performance. Even though LRT is heavily subsidized with public money, it refuses to tell the public what that money is being spent on. What does LRT have to hide?

Plenty of things, in fact. In September 1984 the GLC claimed that LRT was about to announce fare increases which would come into effect the following January. LRT denied that any such decision was imminent. Yet less than two weeks later LRT announced that fares would indeed rise in January. As an editorial in the *Standard* commented:

> The first fares-fixing exercise by the new masters of London Transport is not proving a particularly happy one. News of it has trickled out through leaks, more or less shaky denials from London Regional Transport, and then confirmation that the leaks were essentially right after all.

The newspaper added:

> Of explanation there has been little sign. Of consultation, no sign at all.

It is easy to understand why LRT was so secretive about its plans. They included:

- A rise in 'short-hop' bus fares from 20p to 25p – an increase of 25 per cent.
- A rise in children's bus fares from 10p to 15p – a 50 per cent increase.
- A scrapping of cheap travel on Sundays, leading to a 200 per cent increase in the maximum child's fare on the tube, up from 20p to 60p.
- A rise in fares for tube journeys across two zones from 50p to 60p – a 20 per cent increase.

But LRT's announcement was good news for at least one group – better-off people living in the Home Counties. For example, the cost of a daily trip from Ongar to Buckhurst Hill was nearly cut in half, from £2.10 to £1.20. Ratepayers in places such as Ongar are outside the GLC's boundaries and therefore do not contribute to the GLC's subsidy for London Transport. In other words, the reduction in their fares has been achieved at the expense of Londoners.

An even more bizarre part of LRT's package was a freeze on underground fares to Heathrow Central – presumably in the belief that people who can afford an air ticket may somehow be unable to stump up a few pence extra on the tube, while ordinary passengers on London's buses and tube trains can safely be saddled with rises of up to 200 per cent.

LRT also announced that it would introduce a Capitalcard, which passengers could use on British Rail and LRT. But it neglected to mention that this was to be up to 37 per cent more expensive than a similar card which the GLC had intended to introduce.

When LRT was set up in June 1984, the government gave it the following targets:

- A reduction of 2.5 per cent in its costs *in real terms* (i.e. after inflation) every year for 'the next few years'.
- A reduction in its subsidy from £190 million in 1984 to £95 million in 1987.

LRT has lost no time in putting London's transport back on the road to decline. It has already announced a 3 per cent reduction in bus services from February 1985, and further cuts are planned. It is hard to realize what effect these cuts will have if one relies only on the bland statements put out by LRT. Here, for instance, is all that LRT had to say about its changes to route 275:

> Because of the poor use made of this service, route 275 is to be withdrawn on Sundays. Alternative facilities from Walthamstow to Claybury Hospital are available by route 206.

It sounds harmless enough – but it tells only half the story. It does not mention that the 206 operates only in the afternoons. Nor does it reveal that this change will mean that there is no access to Claybury from the east or the west, even though Claybury is a specialist psychiatric hospital and visitors could therefore be expected from wide areas of London.

All passengers will be affected by the cuts in bus services, but as women rely more on buses than men do, they will suffer more. In particular, there are several reductions in evening services – a time when women are especially vulnerable to assault. Black people will be badly affected as well, since a relatively high proportion of them are employed on shiftwork and thus depend on evening and weekend buses.

LRT also plans to increase the use of 'one-person-operated' buses, replacing the traditional open-platform vehicles. These buses are slower and more difficult to manoeuvre. They also spend more time at bus stops (since the driver has to collect the fares) and prevent passengers from getting on or off when the bus is stopped in congested traffic. The removal of conductors will be a great inconvenience to passengers who need assistance when boarding or alighting, notably pensioners, disabled people and women with small children.

Another effect of introducing more 'driver-only' buses is, of course, to put bus conductors out of work.

More than 500 conductors will lose their jobs as a result of the 'driver-only' conversions that have been announced so far – and LRT has made it clear that many other bus routes will lose their conductors before long. A high proportion of these conductors will be black people – at a time when jobs for black people in London are already scarce.

Women will also suffer, being deprived of one of the few secure and relatively well-paid jobs available to them. About 20 per cent of LRT's bus conductors are women, compared with less than 1 per cent of bus drivers. Needless to say, it is highly unlikely that women conductors who are made redundant will find alternative employment at the same level of pay.

The other disadvantage of 'one-person-operated' buses is the risk of vandalism. With the driver effectively trapped in the driving seat, and with no conductor, gangs of hoodlums can roam the upper deck at will, robbing and threatening passengers – possibly even raping or murdering them. All the evidence suggests that passengers, particularly on late-night journeys, appreciate the presence of a conductor. But the customers' wishes are no longer LRT's main consideration.

The same is true on the underground, where LRT is speeding up the introduction of 'one-person-operated' trains. As with the buses, this is being done in the name of 'efficiency' and 'economy'. But as with the buses, the effect on staff and passengers could be disastrous. People who are afraid of assault will no longer be able to travel in the guard's carriage, since there will be no guard there. Protection against other hazards of tube travel will also be reduced. If there is a fire in the middle of a train, the driver will be unable to get through to the rear carriages – where the guard used to be to make sure that passengers do not climb on to the live rail.

This is not some sort of speculative fantasy: fires on the underground are all too common. In 1984 LRT had more than 100 reports of rubbish smouldering on the line, which was extinguished before it could spread. There have been four major fires in tube tunnels in the last ten years – at Finsbury Park in 1976, at Goodge Street in 1981, at Bounds Green in 1982 and at Oxford Circus in 1984. There have also been other accidents, the most horrifying of which was the Moorgate tube disaster of 1975. As recently as December 1984, one tube train crashed into another at Kilburn.

As long as accidents like that can happen – and the underground will *never* be 100 per cent safe – there will be a need for guards on trains. One of the guards' jobs is to check that all passengers have boarded safely and that the doors are properly closed before giving the driver the signal to pull out of the station. On the routes where LRT has experimented with 'guardless' trains there has been a problem with drivers shutting the doors when passengers are only half-way in, because a driver can't see all the way down a curved platform.

It's true that television monitors are being installed on platforms to overcome this problem, but they have already shown a worrying propensity to break down. In any case, they are of no use once the driver has pulled into the tunnel. As one guard told *Time Out* magazine in October 1984:

> Only last week, I had to stop the train when a
> drunk parted the doors as the train was pulling
> away. If the train had been driver-only, it
> would have just pulled away at speed and he
> would have been smashed into the tunnel wall.

Will LRT reconsider its plans in view of these dangers? It has shown no sign of doing so. The needs of employees and passengers no longer seem to matter very much. The whole philosophy of London Transport has been changed.

Until 1984 it was a service, scrutinized and controlled by an elected local authority and therefore accountable (to a certain extent) to Londoners. Thus the people of London could actually influence the behaviour of London Transport – as they did in 1981, for instance, when they voted for a party whose manifesto had promised fare cuts. The fare cuts were duly introduced. (What the GLC had not bargained for, of course, was that judges might choose to override the wishes of the electorate.)

Now, however, LRT is no longer a service but a nationalized industry, accountable only to the Secretary of State for Transport, Nicholas Ridley – who has no particular duty to consider the views of Londoners when planning LRT's future. Although nominally in 'public ownership', LRT, like other nationalized industries, is not responsible to the public at all – certainly not to its workforce or its customers. Instead, like other nationalized industries, it must follow the whims and prejudices of the government of the day. The attitudes of the present government to nationalized industries are simple:

○ They should sack staff and take other 'cost-cutting' measures.
○ They should be privatized as far as possible.

Both these principles are already being put into practice at London Regional Transport. A few days before Christmas in 1984, LRT announced that it would cut 3,000 jobs – 5 per cent of all staff – in the following year. And plans for privatization were already well advanced: in October 1984, LRT invited private operators to submit tenders for 13 of its bus routes. These represented only 1 per cent of LRT's total bus routes, but as Ian Phillips, LRT's board member for finance and planning, said: 'The 13 routes have been selected as a first step in the process.'

'The process' is the business of hiving off the rest of LRT's bus routes. No business operator will want to tender for routes which are unprofitable but are nevertheless a valuable public service, so these routes will eventually be abolished. Meanwhile, the operators will cut their costs to the bone on the tenders for the profitable routes so that their bids are the lowest – and therefore the likeliest to win.

Since the private contractors will be obliged to charge the same fares as LRT, the scope for cost-cutting will be limited. The two most likely victims are

51

○ Vehicle maintenance
○ Staff wages

The first will put passengers in danger; the second will hurt the workforce.

On past experience of 'privatization' of council services, both seem likely. Some private contractors who take over councils' tasks – waste collection, for instance – have poor records as employers and take a rather casual attitude to health and safety. Such practices are inevitable when something which was previously a service becomes a business, to be run on 'economic' lines.

Thus the streets of London will become an adventure playground for private bus companies, as they engage in cut-throat competition for the most lucrative routes. A rerun of the 1920s, in fact, when bus companies fought for passengers in busy areas while ignoring 'unprofitable' routes and not bothering with safety standards. It was precisely because this system was so chaotic that the Road Traffic Act was passed in 1930, to regulate the bus operators and remove the element of competition.

All that is now to be changed. If the government gets its way and achieves full 'deregulation' of buses, London's streets will come to resemble Brands Hatch during a particularly rough Grand Prix. Small wonder that Nicholas Ridley has acquired the nickname 'Mr Toad'.

Disabling the disabled
On 24 August 1984 London Regional Transport issued an innocuous-looking press release headed 'Later Start Restored for Handicapped Persons' Free Travel'. The use of the word 'restored' gave the impression that LRT was doing something beneficial for people with disabilities – an utterly misleading impression. For it turned out that LRT was ending the concession whereby disabled people could use their free-travel passes on buses and tubes from 9a.m. on weekdays. From September, disabled people were not allowed to use their permits until 9.30 – a petty-minded act and a serious inconvenience to many disabled travellers.

To be fair, it wasn't entirely LRT's fault. The London Boroughs Association, which was responsible for administering the scheme, had told LRT to move the starting-time from 9 to 9.30 because the additional half-hour was a period of 'special and unacceptable risk for the disabled'. This mysterious pronouncement was certainly not supported by the Greater London Association for the Disabled, who were thoroughly disappointed by the change. As Dave Wetzel, who chairs the GLC's Transport Committee, put it at the time:

> I am disgusted by this example of the
> paternalistic attitude of able-bodied people
> towards those with disabilities. Surely they are
> quite capable of deciding for themselves when
> it is safe to travel?

Before it was deprived of its responsibility for London Transport, the GLC was taking action to make access to buses and tubes easier for disabled people. When the London Regional Transport Bill was going through parliament an amendment was proposed, with all-party support, which would have made LRT responsible for transport for the disabled. It failed. Instead, the government introduced an amendment which merely required LRT to 'have regard' to the needs of people with disabilities – a vague enough remit to ensure that little or nothing is done about it.

Nevertheless, disabled people in London are much more mobile today than they were five years ago. For a long time they were housebound and invisible unless they were lucky enough to have a specially adapted car or a mobility allowance. In the words of Val Bassett, co-ordinator of Wandsworth Community Transport:

> The disabled are ratepayers, too, but their
> disability denies them access to London's
> public transport that the fit and mobile can
> use. A pensioner's bus pass is no help if
> you can't get outside your own front door or

don't have the strength to stand in a bus
queue.

Wandsworth Community Transport is one of two dozen
'dial-a-ride' services for the disabled which have started
since 1981 with money from the GLC. "Dial-a-ride' offer
door-to-door transport for the disabled in special buses
for no more than the cost of a normal bus fare. The GLC
has spent £3,500,000 on funding these services and a
Federation of London Dial and Rides – by no means an
excessive sum considering that 200,000 Londoners are
disabled. Dial-a-rides are in action for 15 hours a day, 364
days a year (only on Christmas Day does the service
stop).

In addition to this, the GLC offers subsidized taxi
fares to disabled people. The Taxicard began as an
experiment in one borough in January 1983 but by
October 1984 it had become a city-wide institution with
33,000 members. Using a Taxicard, a disabled person can
obtain a large discount on the fare in any of 4,500
licensed radio-controlled black cabs.

If the government abolishes the GLC, these schemes
will become the responsibility of the borough councils.
Some boroughs – the tight-fisted ones – will have no
desire to continue with dial-a-rides and Taxicards. Others
may want to keep the schemes going but – because of
rate-capping – will be unable to do so. What is certain is
that many disabled people will become housebound
once again.

One for the road
At the moment the GLC is responsible for maintaining
and improving London's 900-mile network of main roads,
except for 143 miles of trunk roads which are controlled
by central government. If the GLC is abolished, the
Secretary of State for Transport will take direct control
of another 65 miles of roads – thus making them trunk
roads too – as well as maintaining reserve powers over
another 305 miles of London roads. These 'reserve
powers' will undoubtedly be used, as we shall see later.

Thus, in effect, control of the capital's highways will have passed from the directly elected council to the Secretary of State – who could perfectly well be the MP for Orkney and Shetland or maybe Penzance, and who therefore has no automatic interest in the fate of Londoners.

Before proceeding any further, it is worth explaining what a trunk road is. It is a route mainly intended to cater for long-distance through-traffic – including lorries. If a road is 'trunked', maps and signposts are changed to encourage traffic on to that road. If you live on a trunk road you soon know all about it from the noise and fumes of the traffic. But you are not entitled to any compensation.

Nor is there any guarantee that the government will stop there. All the indications are that it intends to widen many trunk roads – making 'general improvements', as the government charmingly puts it – and possibly even turn some of them into urban motorways.

In November 1984 Nicholas Ridley gave a taste of what was to come when he announced that he had commissioned 'exploratory studies' of four areas – part of the South Circular, the area between the A1 and A102 in north-east London, the corridor through London to the south coast, and a relief road to replace the Earl's Court one-way system. In his bland statement, Ridley said only that: 'Action to tackle unpleasant conditions on London's overcrowded roads is long overdue.'

What was slightly odd about his action was that he was jumping the gun: he didn't actually control the roads for which he was commissioning 'studies'. Even if the GLC is abolished, he won't get his hands on them until 1986. Yet by his announcement he cast a blight over vast areas of London, putting in doubt the future of half a million houses which lie near the roads, as well as numerous businesses and development schemes.

If the GLC disappears, we can expect many more schemes of the same kind – some of them revivals of discredited plans from the 1960s, when urban motorways were fashionable. And these 'improvements' will not be confined to the 65 miles of trunk roads which the government is grabbing, for it is also taking reserve powers over a whole new category of roads – 'designated' roads. The Secretary of State for Transport can 'designate' *any* road (not just former GLC roads) at *any* time and can then veto any proposal from the borough owning the road which might restrict 'or otherwise regulate' traffic. The power even extends to a non-designated road which 'directly affects' traffic or parking on a designated road.

Thus the government will not only be taking effective control of *all* the roads formerly owned by the GLC, but it will also take over roads which have until now been the responsibility of the boroughs. It is worth remembering that the government claims that its intention in killing the GLC is to devolve power *to* the boroughs.

It's true that some powers will go to the borough councils – but only in theory. The theory is that each of the 33 authorities (the City plus 32 boroughs) will become a 'highways and traffic authority', in charge of traffic lights, pedestrian crossings, parking, one-way systems, bus lanes, cycle lanes and many other tasks which are currently performed for the whole of London by the GLC.

In practice, however, many of these jobs will be taken over by the Secretary of State. This is because traffic problems in London are not neatly confined within the boundaries of individual boroughs. So the borough councils will not be able to discharge their new duties properly unless they can co-operate with one another. On past form it seems unlikely that they can. It is for this reason that a strategic authority like the GLC is so essential for a sane transport system in London: it can take a general view of the needs of Londoners as a whole, rising above parochial squabbles between different boroughs, who are bound to have conflicts of interest from time to time. Two examples make the point:

○ Half the **Charing Cross Road** falls within the borders of Westminster City Council; the other half is in Camden. At the moment the road carries one-way traffic north from Trafalgar Square to Tottenham Court Road. But Camden wants to introduce a south-bound bus lane and cycle lane. Westminster Council is 'absolutely against' the plan. Deadlock. The GLC's function is to find a solution to such disagreements.

○ The proposed **Hayes by-pass** has always been supported by Hillingdon Council since it will take through-traffic away from the town centre; Ealing Council, on the other hand, was not so enthusiastic since the by-pass would bring more traffic into Ealing. The dispute was settled by the GLC, which decided in favour of the by-pass. If the GLC goes, the Secretary of State will have to decide. And who will pay for it? The by-pass benefits more than one borough, but if the GLC is abolished, Hillingdon will have to meet the whole cost itself – which it can't afford. The by-pass will then have to be scrapped, and the traffic problems of Hillingdon will be as bad as ever.

There are many other cases where boroughs have been at loggerheads over particular schemes. Until now the GLC, representing the people of London, has been able to arbitrate. What will happen if the GLC goes?

The government's Bill to abolish the GLC makes interesting reading on this point. What it amounts to is a massive concentration of power in the hands of the Secretary of State for Transport, Nicholas Ridley. The Bill says that the Transport Secretary 'may issue guidance' to boroughs on virtually all their responsibilities for traffic control. If, in his 'opinion', a borough takes action contrary to that 'guidance' he can then direct the borough to take specified steps within a specified period. If (again in the Transport Secretary's 'opinion') the borough does not obey the direction, Mr Ridley can then himself arrange for the work to be done and charge the borough for it.

❝ **Without a London-wide authority to take a more detached view, individual boroughs would be pressurized by residents' groups to install such traffic control measures as width restrictions and zebra crossings. However, even these relatively minor schemes can influence traffic flows in neighbouring boroughs . . . In reality the minister himself would have to make the decision. Does he really want to take the responsibility for determining detailed London traffic schemes? ❞**

GLC Conservative Group, January 1984

Moreover, if the Transport Secretary 'considers' that two or more boroughs have made 'inadequate' arrangements for traffic-control systems, he can take over the scheme himself and charge the boroughs. And, of course, if one borough objects to a road scheme proposed by another borough, the decision on whether or not the scheme goes ahead will be taken by . . . our old friend, the Secretary of State. Mr Ridley clearly has a busy time ahead of him.

Few people are fooled by the government's claim that the GLC's responsibilities for traffic and roads will pass to the boroughs. Certainly experts and professionals are under no illusions about what will actually happen – which is why they have been almost unanimously hostile to the government's proposals. For instance, the British Road Federation and the Movement for London sent a joint message to the government in which they argued:

An administrative body with responsibility to oversee transport and strategic planning policies throughout the Greater London area is necessary.

They added:

BRF/MFL do not consider the proposal to reassign traffic management powers from the GLC to the 32 London boroughs and the City of London to be capable of providing sufficient mobility for road traffic within and through the London area, including the effective operation of public road transport.

The London Transport Passengers' Committee, an independent statutory body, told the government:

We are unconvinced that to leave such crucial areas of responsibility to the voluntary co-operation of 33 highly dissimilar and individual authorities (which have seldom if ever reached unanimity on any other matter) will result in the formulation of any coherent or generally agreed policies, let alone their implementation.

The Institution of Highways and Transport was brief and to the point:

The institution is seriously concerned that the proposals of the government for the future do not indicate any realization of the importance of such a central focus of authority and resources.

The prestigious Royal Town Planning Institute was even blunter:

In our view the present system is superior to the White Paper proposals, which provide immense opportunity for delay, inaction and disagreement and confusion.

Even the Freight Transport Association, which has spent the past year denouncing the GLC's proposal for a night-time ban on heavy lorries coming through London, has told the government that the council is irreplaceable:

> The establishment of the GLC has meant that
> ample resources have been available over the
> years to employ highly expert professional
> staff on specific issues. In London, and most of
> the Metropolitan Counties, there are very
> experienced engineers who have made it their
> job to understand industry and its transport
> needs. While in most cases it clearly would not
> be possible to retain these teams intact, it
> would be a great pity if such a reorganization
> allowed this expertise to be lost to industry
> and local government.

The testimonial from the Freight Transport Association
is particularly impressive because, as mentioned above,
it has no great reason to love the GLC at the moment. But
the lorry ban is, in fact, a good example of the kind of
problem for which a London-wide authority is necessity.
There were two clearly defined interests in conflict with
each other.

On the one hand were the **thousands of Londoners** who hadn't had a decent night's sleep for years
because of the juggernauts rumbling past their windows
throughout the small hours.

On the other hand were the many **shops and
businesses** which claimed that they had to have goods
delivered to them by lorry in the early hours of the
morning. Supermarkets, for instance, said that they were
dependent on having bread, milk and so on in time to put
it on the shelves before the doors opened for custom.

The GLC was obliged to do its customary impersona-
tion of Solomon. First, it set up an inquiry chaired by
Derek Wood QC, who suggested that the GLC should
consider a weekend and night-time ban on heavy lorries.

There was then a long period of consultation and
discussion. Finally, in December 1984, the GLC's
transport committee voted to ban lorries over 16.5
tonnes from most London roads between 9p.m. and 7a.m.

on weekdays. At weekends, the ban would apply from 1p.m. on Saturday until 7a.m. on Monday.

But the ban was by no means as fearsome as some hauliers claimed. For one thing, the GLC had excluded from the ban a network of roads servicing some of London's biggest industrial estates. It also agreed to issue exemption permits to lorries which could not avoid using inner-city roads at night – such as those making essential deliveries. Lorries which had business in central London would be relatively unaffected. But the ban would stop juggernauts driving through London on their way to or from the coast.

The GLC also said that exemption permits could be issued to lorries which were fitted with 'hush kits' – a special device developed by the GLC and costing only a few hundred pounds. The hush kits give results only one decibel louder than the government's proposed noise limits for lorries. The difference is that hush kits can be fitted straightaway, whereas the government does not expect its limits to come into effect until the late 1990s.

As this suggests, central government is less bothered by the problem caused by lorries than the GLC is . Hence Nicholas Ridley's promise that he would quash the GLC's lorry ban as soon as it was introduced. To be sure, the ban might have had its faults – what compromise doesn't? – but at least it was an attempt to do something to relieve the misery of thousands of Londoners who live on lorry routes. It seems that the government would rather do nothing. Even the *Standard,* a newspaper which doesn't usually have much sympathy for the GLC, roundly condemned the Transport Secretary:

> He really should think again himself about what Londoners want. There is not the faintest doubt that most people, if asked, would welcome and applaud every possible effort to corral the juggernaut, with its noise, its stink and its danger.

The *Standard* pointed out that there was something

more important at stake, too:

> The affair clearly underlines the need for a
> London-wide representative voice after the
> GLC goes. The government, as we can see,
> would never contemplate a London-wide lorry
> ban. It is a scheme only a London-wide elected
> body could hope to implement.

Precisely. And that's why the government is so determined to end the London-wide elected body – so that it can allow lorries to rampage round London with impunity. The government's obsession with encouraging lorries is not shown merely by its opposition to the GLC's lorry ban. It is also evident in Nicholas Ridley's 'exploratory' road-building studies, which mark a shift of emphasis from encouraging heavy traffic to go *round* London wherever possible, to making access easier for lorries *coming into* the centre of the city.

The GLC tends to be wary of huge road-building programmes as a solution to London's traffic problems, since research shows that these extra roads will simply attract even more traffic into town and leave the congestion as bad as ever. However, if the GLC is convinced that a new road is necessary, as a strategic authority it makes sure that this will meet the needs of all road users – buses, bicycles and pedestrians as well as cars and lorries. The government has made it clear that if the GLC is abolished, in future only cars and lorries will be taken into consideration.

We have already seen how the government has set about dismembering the capital's bus service. But abolition would also mean the likely end of special schemes for cyclists and pedestrians which have been introduced in recent years.

Walking is often the quickest way of getting about in London, but it is made dangerous and difficult by heavy traffic. More than half the people killed in road accidents are pedestrians. The GLC has created a number of new pedestrian areas, and anyone who has walked through

Leicester Square or the Covent Garden piazza will know what a difference is made by the absence of traffic. More pedestrian crossings have been installed, and since January 1985 there has been a London-wide ban on parking on the pavements. If the GLC disappears, will these initiatives continue? It seems unlikely: the government's plans published so far show no recognition that pedestrians even exist.

The omens are no better for bicyclists, since the government's attitude – 'Let them drive cars,' as Marie Antoinette might have put it – makes no allowance for the fact that more and more people these days prefer to travel by bike, for reasons of economy, health and convenience. In 1981 a Cycle Project Team was formed within the GLC and given the task of designing cycle lanes on major routes. By the end of 1984, 25 such schemes had already been opened and many more were in the pipeline: the eventual target was a 1,000-mile network of cycle routes in London. Lanes already in use include the Ambassador Route from Paddington to Chelsea (during 1985 it will be extended into Battersea Park), cycle lanes on Waterloo Bridge and the Somerstown Route from Camden to Holborn.

All this will probably come to a halt if the GLC is abolished. Cyclists will then have to take their chances competing with heavy vehicles on crowded roads – which will inevitably lead to more accidents. Of course, it is possible that the government does indeed intend to encourage the building of cycle lanes – but if so, why hasn't it been mentioned anywhere in the many publications which the government has produced in connection with the GLC's abolition? Perhaps another part of the government's policy for transport in London is the belief that pigs might fly. Or, to put it in the kind of language which Whitehall understands, that porcine aviation is viable.

3 No place like home

Past experience of the reluctance of the outer boroughs to participate voluntarily in what they regard as a purely inner-London problem gives us no confidence that they will accept responsibility for providing for single homeless people if the GLC is abolished.

Catholic Housing Aid Service

London has a huge housing crisis. Nowhere else in Britain is it so difficult to find anywhere to live. A few statistics will show the scale of the crisis:

○ 240,000 homes in London are unfit for human habitation
○ 500,000 are in serious disrepair
○ 240,000 lack basic amenities
○ 130,000 people are living in overcrowded conditions
○ 20,000 families are made homeless every year
○ Many thousands more have to sleep in shabby hostels or on the streets
○ 240,000 people are on the waiting list for council housing in London

The burden of trying to do something about these dreadful conditions falls largely on local councils and the GLC. Not only is there an urgent need for more house-building; there is also a massive job of work to be done renovating the existing houses and flats which are scarcely habitable. One home in four in London is either unfit for human habitation, lacking in basic amenities

74% OF LONDONERS ARE AGAINST ABOLISHING THE GLC. WHAT'S THE GOVERNMENT DOING ABOUT IT?

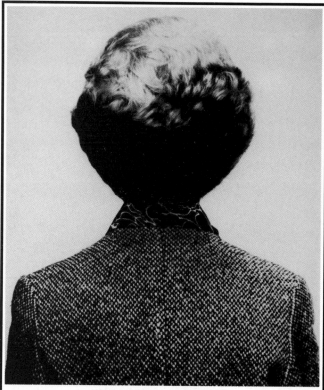

THAT'S WHAT.

The final stage in the Government's plans to abolish the GLC was announced in the Queen's speech yesterday.

Their Abolition Bill goes before Parliament this session.

If it's passed, the organisation that's been running London democratically for almost a century will be scrapped.

And most of its responsibilities won't go to the boroughs as the Government claims but to Whitehall quangos and joint boards which aren't directly elected.

All this will happen in spite of the fact that it's against the wishes of an overwhelming 74% of Londoners.

Understandably, they want to keep the right to decide for themselves at the ballot box who runs London.

The Government obviously isn't interested in what they want.

It's pushing ahead with its proposals because it suits them to.

It's an insult to the people of London.

And it's up to every MP who believes in democratic government to vote against it.

In a democracy a government is there to act on behalf of the people who elected it.

Not to turn its back and ignore them. SAY NO TO NO SAY.

IF YOU HAVE ANY COMPLAINTS WHEN THE GLC GOES, YOU'LL BE TALKING TO WHITEHALL.

SAY NO TO NO SAY.

NEXT YEAR ALL LONDONERS' VOTES GO THE SAME WAY.

If the Government has its way there won't be any GLC elections to vote in next year. **SAY NO TO NO SAY.**

IF THE GLC GOES, WHITEHALL MOVES IN.

London is better off run by Londoners, not Whitehall. **SAY NO TO NO SAY.**

HOW MUC
SQUEEZE OU

If the Transport Bill becon will go up 20%. Kill

COME IN NUMBER 9 YOUR TIME IS UP

If the Transport Bill becomes law, services will be cut.
Kill the Bill. Phone 633 4400

GLC
Working together for London

WILL THEY ... OF THE TUBE?

... London Transport fares
... Bill. Phone 633 4400

GLC
Working for London

AFTER 50 YEARS, IS THIS THE END OF THE LINE?

LONDON TRANSPORT

The Transport Bill means higher fares and fewer services.
Kill the Bill. Phone 633 4400

GLC
Working for London

Don't litter Lon

Make Lon

LONDON'S PARKS COULD BECOME MASS GRAVEYARDS LIKE

LONDON AGAINST RACISM

IF YOU'RE NOT PART OF THE SOLUTION, YOU'RE PART OF THE PROBLEM.

You've got the power to challenge the damaging effects of racism. Use it!

RACISM: Better off without it. RACISM

...ndon's parks **nuclear free.**

...THE EVENT OF A NUCLEAR STRIKE

GLC
Working for London and Peace

THERE'S ONE LONDONER THE GLC IS TAKING TO THE CLEANERS.

For more information ring 633 4400.

If the banks had bothered to look at tomorrow's possibilities and not just today's balance sheets.

If the company had been helped to go forwards to meet new demands by developing new products.

If management had permitted the shop floor to make a real contribution.

If the Government had given a damn.

Maybe many hundreds of business enterprises would have been saved and thousands of today's unemployed would still be at work.

Fortunately for London, there's the GLC, and we give a lot more than a damn.

That's why we've set up the Greater London Enterprise Board (GLEB) to help ensure there's a real industrial future for London with worthwhile, long term jobs for Londoners.

And that means making sure that viable businesses are not allowed to go to the wall.

So far GLEB has helped hundreds of business concerns and secured thousands of Londoners' jobs for the future.

If you'd like to know more, call us. 01-633 4400.

GLC WORKING FOR LONDON.

IT NEED NEVER HAVE HAPPENED.

such as a bathroom or an inside lavatory, or in serious disrepair.

Matters are even worse in the private sector. Over half the homes owned by private landlords are unsatisfactory, and 200,000 owner-occupied properties are now in serious disrepair.

The new Greater London Development Plan provides for the building of 200,000 new homes in all tenures over the next ten years, most of which would be houses with gardens. The plan also calculated that 950,000 properties – both private and council-owned – would have to be renovated over the next ten years.

All this would be in addition to the GLC's many other tasks connected with housing. One of the myths constantly repeated by ministers is that the GLC 'no longer has any housing responsibilities.' Nothing could be further from the truth.

The GLC has the biggest programme of renovation to council homes in the country. It is responsible for modernizing, improving and repairing the 40,000 homes which it still owns itself, as well as the 155,000 homes formerly within its ownership which were transferred to the borough councils at the end of the 1970s.

When the boroughs were asked by the government to take over these GLC properties they made it clear that they could do so only if the GLC promised to bring them up to modern standards. No borough council could afford to pay for the work itself.

The GLC duly gave its promise. It undertook to spend £1,000 million on the properties. By 1992 they would all be modernized. As the 1992 deadline suggests, it is a hefty task, involving a wide range of work:

○ Some inter-war council estates were built with a bath in the kitchen; they now need a separate bathroom.
○ Some old flats need a complete package of improvements, consisting of a new kitchen, bathroom and central heating.
○ Technical problems on estates – such as damp

penetration – are remedied after scientific
surveys.
○ Many properties need a new roof and new
window-frames.

Alongside these works, the GLC has developed several
ways of improving the safety and quality of life on the
estates, particularly for women, who spend more time in
and around the home than men do and therefore suffer
disproportionately from bad housing conditions and
vandalism. These measures provide that:

○ Strong doors with entryphone systems are put
at main entrances, with floodlights installed
overhead.
○ Fire-doors are placed at regular intervals along
corridors, both to stop fire spreading and to
prevent skateboarders, rollerskaters and so
forth from speeding along public passages.
○ Specially strengthened front doors, built to
resist even the most determined intruder, are
installed on estates where break-ins are
common.
○ Internal and external walls are cleaned by the
GLC's special anti-graffiti squad.
○ Courtyards are tidied and flowers, shrubs and
trees are planted around the estate.

In addition to its work on council estates, the GLC also
pays for improvements to private housing. This is done
mainly through taking a decaying locality and designating it as a Housing Action Area or a General Improvement
Area. These have been declared in 17 places in Inner
London, covering about 13,000 homes.

They are areas of crumbling housing, usually
privately rented and owner-occupied. They contain
people living in appallingly overcrowded conditions and
lacking even basic amenities. Many of the families living
there are ethnic minorities. Elderly people, too, are often
found in large numbers in these areas. Of course, they

cannot afford the repair work.

When a place becomes a Housing Action Area or a General Improvement Area, a GLC team moves in and residents are encouraged to apply for improvement grants. The results are impressive: people who have for years lived in squalid, crumbling housing suddenly find themselves equipped with a new roof or central heating, a new bathroom or kitchen.

The GLC only declares a place to be a HAA or GIA at the invitation of the borough in whose boundaries it falls. Most of the boroughs which have invited the GLC to declare these areas have said that they would not otherwise have the resources to improve the areas.

So what will happen if the GLC is abolished? The job of improving and renovating housing – both private and council-owned – will be left to the borough councils. To pay for it, they will need a huge increase in their allocation of money for housing from central government.

Will that increase be forthcoming? The government is careful not to commit itself, so it must be judged on its past record. Between 1979 and 1984 the amount of money made available for investment in public housing in London was *halved* – at a time of desperate housing crisis. And at the end of 1984 the government announced a change in the rules governing local authority investment, wiping out £1.2 billion worth of potential house-building for the next year. That was on top of a cut of £65 million in housing allocations announced a few weeks earlier – a cut which was hailed as a 'victory' for Patrick Jenkin, on the grounds that the Treasury had originally demanded a cut of no less than £600 million.

None of this is likely to make the boroughs feel confident that the government will step in to fill the gap left if the GLC goes. The present government has made it plain that it doesn't like council housing. As the *Times* reported when the government changed the rules governing housing investment: 'The rules are a further step towards the elimination of council house building.' The government would take that as a compliment. It seems to believe that no new council houses should be started, and existing council houses should be sold – hence its 'right to buy' campaign.

This dream of a nation of owner-occupiers – or 'men of property', as Margaret Thatcher likes to call them, perhaps because she doesn't believe women ought to own property – is all very well. But it ignores the facts of life.

The average price of a home for a first-time buyer in London is over £30,000. To be able to afford that, the buyer will first have to raise a deposit – maybe £4,000. Even if she or he can raise that sum, there is then the business of obtaining a mortgage. Normally, building societies will give mortgages of no more than two and a half times your salary. This would mean that the prospective buyer would have to be earning at least £10,000 a year to stand any chance of buying a home. And although it may come as news to some ministers, most Londoners do not earn £10,000 a year.

Since the government is determined to do away with council housing, what are people supposed to do if they cannot buy a home? The only alternative is to rent one privately. Anyone who has ever tried to rent a house or flat in London will know that this is not a simple matter. You rush out to buy the first edition of the evening paper and pore over the classified advertisements. Most of the flats are impossibly expensive, but perhaps you find one or two that are just affordable. You ring the number given, only to find that you're five minutes too late. Or perhaps you go round to the flat and find it riddled with damp and lacking basic amenities.

The problem is particularly bad in central London. For instance, the North Kensington Housing Action Centre in Ladbroke Grove, which is funded by the GLC, recently conducted a survey which found that the rent for double bedsits in the area was £43 a week, while the weekly cost of a one-bedroomed furnished flat might be £98. The local council's top limit for a private rent paid by a tenant who needs housing benefit is £32 a week, but it is doubtful if there are *any* flats in North Kensington where the rent is £32 a week.

Those who can find nowhere to go join the growing number of London's homeless. Every year 20,000 families are accepted as homeless by London's councils and put up in temporary accommodation such as bed-and-breakfasts. This does not include the many thousands of single people in London who also have nowhere to stay. Some of them may move into one of the decrepit Victorian hostels which cater for such people; others will sleep on the pavement or on a park bench.

Single homeless people are helped by the GLC in a number of ways. As well as trying to help rehouse them itself, the council also gives money to other groups which help the homeless.

For instance, the Piccadilly Advice Centre in Piccadilly Circus underground station specializes in advising youngsters who have come to London in search of work and have discovered that the streets are not paved with gold. Many of the youngsters who come to the centre have arrived in London with savings of £50 or perhaps £100, under the impression that they will find a flat for £15 a week. If the centre was not there to help them find a bed for the night and to advise them on jobs, flats, state benefits and so on, many of these youngsters would probably drift into sleeping rough. And, as the television documentary *Johnny Go Home* showed, young newcomers adrift in London are in constant danger of being exploited by villains.

> **❝ The GLC still provides an important mechanism for ensuring that the greatest share of available resources goes to the areas of greatest need. Being directly elected, it can claim with authority to speak on behalf of London as a whole on housing issues. ❞**
>
> Response by Shelter to
> *Streamlining the Cities*

Another organization which seeks to help homeless young people in London is the New Horizon Youth

Centre in Covent Garden. It, too, depends on GLC funds for its existence. More than 3,000 people visit New Horizon's day centre every year. Their average age is just 22.

London has a number of large, old hostels for the homeless which were built in the nineteenth century and are in urgent need of replacement. By historical accident they are located in only a few boroughs. This would mean that without the GLC those boroughs would be lumbered with the whole burden of dealing with homelessness. Other boroughs, on past form, would do nothing about meeting the needs of single homeless people. As SHAC, the London Housing Aid Centre, puts it:

> One of the most important and valuable
> functions of a strategic authority is the ability
> to take action on behalf of groups of people
> who do not necessarily receive adequate
> priority from their local authority, possibly
> because of local political hostility. Provision
> for the single homeless is perhaps the most
> notable example of a need which has all too
> often been ignored by local councils. 'Someone
> ought to do something, but we don't want to
> take the lead because it would make us a
> magnet for people like that' is a response
> which has been heard again and again from
> local councils when pressed to do more for
> single people or those currently living in
> institutions. It is the classic illustration of the
> problem of parochialism which is likely to be
> even more in evidence if the government's
> proposals are enacted.

The GLC funds voluntary groups and housing associations which are of benefit to single homeless people. But it also has a more direct involvement. For instance:

○ In Stamford Street, near Waterloo, the GLC is

establishing a centre for people sleeping rough, along with the specialized medical and support staff needed to run it.

○ In 1983 the GLC set up a Central Outreach Team to provide advice and help to people sleeping rough. The team also collected information which was published in the report *Sleeping Out in Central London*. This in turn was used to set up the Thames Reach Housing Association, which will manage the specialist hostels for the homeless which are due to open in 1985.

○ The GLC has also been involved in the acquisition and running of three Rowton hotels – run-down Victorian relics which accommodate hundreds of homeless people.

○ One of them, Tower House in Tower Hamlets, is now managed by the GLC on behalf of the borough and large investment has taken place to make it bearable pending its replacement.

As well as helping the single homeless, the GLC works for certain groups of homeless people who have special needs – people with a history of alcohol or drug abuse, ex-offenders, people who are vulnerable because of chronic ill-health or who have been discharged from psychiatric hospitals. People with physical disabilities often need specially designed or adapted homes if they are to be able to live independently.

The GLC funds many housing associations and other bodies which provide accommodation for people with these needs. If the government has its way and abolishes the only London-wide housing authority, funding will depend on the boroughs. A study in 1984 by Special Needs Housing Research showed that even if they were willing, most boroughs, threatened by rate-capping, could not take on the cost of this funding.

Nor are the prospects any brighter for other groups who have particular problems with housing – single-parent families, for example, or battered women. Lord

McGregor of Durris, President of the National Council of One-Parent Families, has told the government:

> We fear that the proposed legislation will adversely affect one-parent families, of whom 153,620 live in London.

The GLC provides money for women's refuges in London, too, but there is no likelihood that borough councils would fill the gap left if the GLC were abolished. Accommodation for battered women is a London-wide problem which can only be properly dealt with on a London-wide scale. To quote Southwark Women's Aid:

> We shudder to think what would happen to us and many other voluntary organizations if the GLC no longer existed. We provide refuges for women and children escaping from male violence. Apart from the average 100 women and 250 children who each year pass through our refuges we give advice and support to between 800 and 1,000 other women on similar matters.

One group which will be particularly badly affected if the GLC disappears is the ethnic minorities, who suffer disproportionately from the worst housing conditions in both public and private sectors. They are more likely than anyone else to live in overcrowded or unsatisfactory accommodation. Moreover, they often suffer from direct or indirect discrimination in the allocation of housing, and are subject to racial harassment once they do find a house.

> **❝The problems of London's homeless do not begin and end at borough boundaries. Inter-borough co-ordination can be effective, but often needs to be backed by resources and research from a London-wide agency.❞**
>
> *Community Care* magazine, 30 August 1984

The GLC's position as housing authority for the whole capital allows it to deal with London-wide problems which might otherwise be ignored by many boroughs – from the homelessness of single people to racial harassment, from battered women to disabled people. A classic instance of a task that individual boroughs simply couldn't perform is the GLC's London-wide Mobility Scheme. Occupants of private houses are usually able to move house more easily than council tenants because most council housing is managed within the boundaries of one borough. But mobility is often needed, for many different reasons – a change in employment, a need to be near some ill relation and so on.

As a result of the Greater London Mobility Scheme, 6,000 tenants a year can move from one part of London to another. How on earth could such a scheme be 'devolved to the boroughs' – which, you will recall, is what the government claims is happening to the GLC's functions?

The answer is that it couldn't, as even the government has finally been forced to admit. The Abolition Bill, published in November 1984, includes a little section allowing the Secretary of State to 'confer on himself' the GLC's right to nominate council tenants for transfer under the Mobility Scheme.

Patrick Jenkin is a busy man, yet apparently he will find the time to look into the merits of 6,000 different individual cases every year – on top of all the other duties which he'll have if the GLC is abolished. As with so many of the GLC's functions which the government says will become 'more responsive to local needs' by going to the boroughs, on closer inspection it turns out that Whitehall will be taking charge.

An even more ludicrous state of affairs has arisen in connection with another of the council's housing services. Since 1964 the GLC has built or bought about 3,400 homes outside London, at the seaside or in the country. They are located in 73 towns in 19 counties, ranging from Skegness in Lincolnshire to Illogan in Cornwall. These flats and bungalows are occupied by retired GLC tenants from the London area.

The scheme works to the benefit of all concerned. Many older people like nothing better than the idea of retiring to the seaside. Meanwhile, by moving out of the capital these people release family accommodation in London at reasonable cost, since building costs are lower outside London and the new property is smaller. Thus, the ratepayers gain too, as do people on the council's waiting list.

After abolition, the ownership of these seaside and country homes will be transferred to the local councils in whose borders they happen to be. It is worth emphasizing that these homes have been paid for over the years by the ratepayers of London, to the tune of about £80 million. Yet the government intends to expropriate or confiscate them and hand them over to district councils which have no great interest in easing the pressure on London's housing.

So how will transfers of London tenants to these homes work if the GLC is abolished? The government originally proposed that it would be up to London boroughs to negotiate with the district councils which would own the seaside and country homes after abolition – a suggestion which the GLC Conservative Group described as a 'positively breathtaking' administrative nightmare.

The GLC Conservative Group also pointed out that it would be possible for the district councils to sell the properties under the 'right to buy' scheme, thus dashing any hope that future generations of Londoners might also be able to retire to the countryside.

In the Abolition Bill, the government has wriggled out of the problem in the same way as it extricated itself from difficulties over the Mobility Scheme. The Secretary of State will be able to 'confer on himself' the power to nominate tenants for these homes. Patrick Jenkin is clearly going to have his work cut out interviewing all the thousands of applicants for transfers to seaside and country homes. It is also hard to see, yet again, how this can be described as 'devolving power'. And, in any case, even if Jenkin does nominate tenants for the flats and bungalows, there is no guarantee that the district councils will accept these nominations: they may have sold the properties already.

A final example of the mess that the government has got itself into is Thamesmead. And if you've never heard of Thamesmead, don't feel ashamed; it seems that the government has never heard of it either. Thamesmead is one of the GLC's major achievements in housing. Yet the Abolition Bill doesn't mention it, and gives no clue as to what might happen to it after abolition.

Thamesmead is, in fact, London's new town, an expanse of land 10 miles south of central London. But it is only half-completed. So far £100 million has been spent on it. There are 5,500 public rented dwellings and 1,200 privately owned ones – built by developers such as Laing's on land sold to them by the GLC. The population is 20,000 but when Thamesmead is finished it should be about twice that figure. There are still 350 acres of overgrown land in Thamesmead to be cleared and built on.

Why hasn't the government announced what will happen to Thamesmead? Because the government hasn't a clue. The town could be handed over to Greenwich and Bexley, the two boroughs within whose boundaries it lies. But both boroughs agree that Thamesmead cannot be split: it must stand as one community. Nor is either borough prepared to take on the whole town single-handed. Only an authority as big as the GLC can cope with a project the size of Thamesmead, which is providing desperately needed housing for Londoners.

No doubt Patrick Jenkin will dream up some 'solution' in due course. But there is also no doubt that it will be botched and chaotic. One of the likeliest outcomes is that Thamesmead will be taken from the GLC and put in the hands of an unelected quango. Like most of the GLC's responsibilities, in fact. Perhaps there might be room somewhere at Thamesmead for a small plaque recalling the words of Kenneth Baker, the Local Government Minister, in an interview with the *Standard* on 4 October 1984:

One of the big lies Livingstone's people have told is that the GLC's powers will go to Whitehall. This is simply not true. They will go to the boroughs where power will be closer to the people, not further away.

4 Back to work

The Greater London Enterprise Board should
be allowed to continue. It fills a need in
London where there has been such an erosion
of business activity . . . I am often told that
there are too many venture capital companies
started, and too many Enterprise Boards for the
actual need. It is my belief that we cannot have
too many organizations which are able to
channel our investment funds back to where
they belong – in industry and not in
speculation on the Stock Exchange, the
property market and overseas. If we fail to do
this we will not survive.

*Sir Kenneth Cork, senior partner of leading
accountants Cork Gully, former Lord Mayor of
London and member of the Wilson Committee
which investigated financial institutions*

London's economy is in a state of collapse. Unemployment in London has trebled since 1979, and now stands at over 400,000. London now has the greatest concentration of unemployed people anywhere in the developed world. Until quite recently, local councils were wary of taking part in trying to revitalize industry in their area. They spent money meeting the needs of local inhabitants in many other ways – housing, social services, transport and so on – but one of the most basic needs of all, the need for work, was largely ignored.

The scale of the current crisis and the failure of government measures to combat unemployment have made councils think again. In recent years a number of councils – including the GLC – have decided that jobs and industry should be treated as high priorities. If a local council has more than 400,000 unemployed among the people it is supposed to represent, it can hardly turn its back on them.

The government's plans for abolishing the GLC scarcely mention the work done by the council in this field; nor do they give any clue as to what would happen to it if the GLC disappears. The only reference to it in the White Paper *Streamlining the Cities* was as follows:

> Borough and district councils already have power to assist industry in their areas. The government consider, therefore, that no specific arrangements are required to replace the role of the GLC and the Metropolitan County Councils in assisting local industry and in drawing on the Urban Programme or Urban Development Grants.

This bland paragraph gives the impression that the problem being dealt with is a comparatively trifling one. The task of coping with London's unemployment and industrial decline can simply be left to borough councils. This ignores three facts:

○ The GLC's budget for industry and employment is £70 million – over twice what the government spends on employment projects in London from its Urban Programme.
○ Borough councils are already strapped for cash because of rate-capping and cuts in government grants.
○ The effects of London's economic crisis are not neatly confined within the boundaries of individual boroughs. Nor can the solutions be.

The size of the problem cannot be overstated. There are 32 million square feet of factory space lying empty in

London. Unemployment has quadrupled in just over ten years and could rise much higher in the next ten. Forty per cent of the 100,000 people out of work in Tower Hamlets, Islington, Newham, Lambeth and Southwark are being classified as 'long-term unemployed', compared with 23 per cent five years ago. This 74 per cent increase in long-term unemployment compares with a 30 per cent increase on Merseyside – itself a depressed area. And since 1981 the unemployment rate has been twice as high for black as for white Londoners.

Between 1966 and 1974 London's population fell by 9.4 per cent, but the capital lost 27 per cent of its manufacturing jobs. The trend has continued. By 1981 London had lost 37 per cent – more than one-third – of its manufacturing jobs over the previous ten years.

Until 1966, the loss of jobs in manufacturing industry was more than offset by the creation of jobs in offices and service industries (shops, catering, entertainment, leisure industries and so on). But since then, even the growth in those areas has slowed down, as the table below graphically shows.

London's jobs (in millions)

	1951	1966	1971	1976	1982
Manufacturing	1.55	1.30	1.09	0.83	0.63
Offices	1.56	1.70	1.65	1.78	1.75
Other	1.18	1.43	1.47	1.10	1.00
Total	**4.29**	**4.43**	**4.21**	**3.71**	**3.38**

The Greater London Enterprise Board (GLEB) was set up by the GLC in 1983 to do something about London's collapsing industry. The board is an independent agency accountable to the council, and staffed by professionals. Its function is to invest in long-term jobs and the development of the London economy. In particular, it attempts to identify unused resources and skills, new products and services which would meet the needs of Londoners and new forms of 'social ownership' which would increase people's control over their working lives. Projects meeting the particular employment needs of women, ethnic minorities and people with disabilities are given special consideration. In its first year of existence, GLEB created or saved 2,000 jobs in 116 different enterprises. The direct cost of preserving or creating each job was under £4,500. This represents extremely good value when compared with other forms of investment in employment – or unemployment, for that matter:

○ The average cost to the taxpayer of each unemployed person in Britain is £5,000. And that's only the cost in terms of money: the social and human cost is also high.
○ The average cost of keeping a married couple with two children unemployed for a year is £7,500.
○ The cost of each job created through government schemes such as Enterprise Zones and Development Areas is anywhere between £20,000 and £60,000.
○ The cost of the government subsidy for each job created by Nissan in the UK is £30,000.

One of GLEB's strongest arguments is that there are many potentially successful businesses in London which need investment, yet financial institutions in the City are often unwilling to provide that investment. Once GLEB has invested in a company and proved its worth, other financiers may then be keener to put up money. One example is Whitechapel Computer Works. This was the brainchild of two computer scientists, Bob Newman and Tim Eccles, who wanted to make powerful desk-top computers for scientists. The market in these machines is highly competitive, but Eccles believed that he could produce one which was 'three times cheaper' than its American rivals by getting all the microchip power on one circuit board.

It seemed a good idea. The City wouldn't back it but

GLEB did, investing £125,000 to get Whitechapel Computer Works off the ground, creating 44 jobs. The GLC provided purpose-built premises for the works. At that stage the City decided that it might be prepared to back the venture after all: the banks belatedly came up with £900,000 to fund further developments.

The same thing happened with Airlec, a company developing an automatic, computer-controlled machine for loading freight and luggage at airports. The inventor, Chris Ross, needed cash to build a prototype. None of the traditional sources in the City would help. GLEB stepped in, and within a few months Airlec's machine was on show for the first time at a special exhibition at Gatwick Airport. Airlines throughout the world were showing a strong interest. And so was the City, at last: knowing they were on to a good thing, the banks which had previously refused any assistance were suddenly *asking* if they could lend money to Airlec.

If GLEB hadn't existed, the Airlec machine would still be on the drawing board. As Chris Ross says:

> Before GLEB invested £50,000 in me no one
> else was prepared to do anything. I would go to
> industrialists or banks and they would look
> askance at the idea. They thought it was too
> big a gamble because it has to be built and
> made and is not really a fancy 'sunrise' product.

Airlec and Whitechapel Computer Works are just two of many examples where GLEB's investment has made all the difference. As they suggest, GLEB often has a different sense of priorities from other financial institutions. Its priorities are, in fact, the same as those of the GLC. GLEB and the GLC are particularly concerned to give support to co-operatives, which often find it difficult to get backing from more conventional sources. The London Co-operative Enterprise Board (established by GLEB) has a budget of £1 million, of which 55 per cent is spent on women, ethnic minority groups and people with disabilities who want to set up co-ops.

□ **Women are often barred from better-paid jobs in industry because they haven't had the chance to gain the skills required for those jobs. One group funded by the GLC, Women Enjoy Building, based in west London, has set up a women's building skills training project. The aim is to encourage women in London to develop non-traditional skills through a course introducing them to such trades as carpentry, plumbing, plastering, bricklaying and painting and decorating.**

Most ambitious of all is the GLC and GLEB Industrial Land Development Programme. The project will use 3 million square feet of empty factory space to provide 13,000 jobs.

London's shortage of jobs is, of course, only part of the story. There has also been a collapse in training. Private firms have cut back on apprenticeships while the government is destroying a large part of Britain's – and London's – training infrastructure. There is no point in creating new jobs unless there are skilled women and men able to take on those jobs.

It was for this reason that the Greater London Training Board was set up as a sub-committee of the GLC in 1981. Since then the board has established itself as one of the few agencies which is actually increasing resources for training and promoting equal opportunities. It is already training 2,600 people, including contributing to the cost of 800 apprenticeships.

Over 200 local projects and campaigns have been grant-aided in a move to tap ordinary people's energy and enthusiasm. Priority goes to groups discriminated against in the labour market.

What will happen to all these activities if the GLC is abolished? The answer is that they will be almost entirely wiped out. As the government itself admits, there will be 'no specific arrangements' for replacing the role of the GLC in assisting local industry; and the government's suggestion that borough councils can take over the work if they want to is obviously not meant to be taken seriously.

In fact, the government feels rather uneasy about the way in which councils such as the GLC have taken on the challenge of reversing unemployment and industrial decline. For one thing, this work tends to make people wonder why the government itself isn't doing more to prevent unemployment and the collapse of industry. For another thing, the government doesn't like the priority which the GLC gives to groups such as women or ethnic minorities. The government may grudgingly concede that these groups are at a disadvantage when it comes to finding decent jobs; but it doesn't believe that any special effort is needed to correct this disadvantage.

The future of GLEB is also unclear. As an independent company it would not automatically be dumped into the Thames at the same time as the GLC if the government's Abolition Bill is passed. However, GLEB's ability to continue to intervene in London's economy would depend on whether it could find other sources of money to replace the GLC.

Pension funds and the EEC are the likeliest providers. Although the pension funds may be reluctant to put forward much cash, GLEB has already won some money from the Common Market – £750,000 in 1984, and it expects more in 1985. Even so, this is only a small part of GLEB's £30 million budget. If GLEB could survive, there seems little doubt that it would be less effective than it is at the moment, with the resources of the GLC behind it. And the dole queues would continue to lengthen.

Among those in the queues would be former GLC employees. The government has made it clear all along that part of its purpose in abolishing the GLC is to increase the number of unemployed in London. As Patrick Jenkin said in November 1983:

I expect the proposed reorganization of local government in Greater London . . . to lead to a substantial reduction in staff numbers.

And again in January 1984:

> Economic and efficient management means
> reducing the over-manning [*sic*], the waste and
> the overheads – not cutting the services that
> people need and should have.

He was careful not to specify how many jobs would go,
confining himself to saying that it would be a 'substantial'
number.

By November 1984, however, when the Abolition
Bill was published, another minister in Patrick Jenkin's
department was prepared to commit himself. Sir George
Young, in reply to a parliamentary question, announced
that abolition of the GLC would lead to 'savings of about
3,500 posts'.

Where did this figure come from? There seem to be
two possibilities. One is that Sir George Young dreamed
it up in his bath one morning. The other is that Patrick
Jenkin dreamed it up in *his* bath.

Patrick Jenkin has promised that the cuts in staff
numbers will be achieved by eliminating 'waste' and not
by cutting services. If he keeps his promise, he will find it
hard to do away with anything approaching 3,500 jobs.
For, contrary to the impression which ministers like to
give, the GLC is not some bloated bureaucracy, stuffed
with useless 'pen-pushers'.

☐ **This is not the first time that Patrick
Jenkin has promised to save money by
abolishing an 'unnecessary'
administrative tier and thereby reducing
the number of staff. In 1980, as Secretary
of State for Health and Social Services,
he was responsible for organizing the
abolition of Area Health Authorities. He
implied that this would save millions of
pounds by getting rid of hundreds of**

bureaucrats. The reorganization duly took place in April 1982. But figures published in November 1983 showed that the number of administrative staff actually *increased* by 600 between September 1981 (six months before reorganization) and June 1983.

Even if *all* the GLC's administrators and managers were sacked – and surely even the government doesn't suggest that *none* of them does anything useful – it would only remove just over 1 per cent of the council's total expenditure. Altogether, staff costs account for only 16 per cent of the GLC's budget, compared with 60 per cent for local government as a whole. And a third of the GLC's staff costs comprise just one group – fire-fighters. Out of the 21,611 people employed by the GLC 6,994 are fire-fighters.

So the scope for staff reduction is small – unless services are to be cut. And this is undoubtedly what will actually happen. There is certainly no disputing that the government *can* reduce the number of staff by 3,500 if it wants to – or by any other figure that comes into its head. The Abolition Bill gives the government enormous power to control staffing levels in the authorities which will take over the GLC's functions.

This will mean that thousands of GLC employees – some with a lifetime of service in local government – may be thrown on to the dole. But it will also mean the end of a long tradition whereby the GLC has acted as a notably more enlightened employer than most bodies in London. When the London County Council was created in 1889 one of its first acts was to adopt a 'fair wages and conditions' clause in all contracts let by the council.

Many years later, in 1980, the government encouraged local authorities to drop their insistence that contractors should adhere to fair wages and conditions. The GLC refused. Instead, it radically extended its work in this area. Its 'Contract Compliance' enables the GLC to further its equal opportunities policies by using the council's £700 million purchasing power to ensure that the 20,000 firms which supply goods and services adopt equal opportunities policies in their employment practice to avoid discrimination in recruitment, training, promotion, disciplinary and grievance procedure. Construction firms are also required to carry out the council's policy on health and safety, pay and conditions, trade union rights, direct labour and training. So far 1,000 contractors have been reviewed.

The demands made of contractors are also made of the GLC itself. In 1981 the council adopted a new equal opportunities policy designed to correct the imbalance which put black people and women at a disadvantage. All staff procedures in County Hall – training, discipline, ways of dealing with grievances and so on – were put under close scrutiny to ensure that equality of opportunity was observed. Methods of recruitment and promotion were changed to give a better chance to people who had until then been at a disadvantage.

As a result of the policy, in the period between September 1981 and September 1984 the number of black people employed by the GLC increased by about 27 per cent – from 1,650 to 2,098; and the number of women by 17 per cent – from 3,970 to 4,664.

Another part of the policy was an Accelerated Development Programme to help ethnic minority and women employees who were stuck in junior and clerical posts for long periods with little prospect of advancement. It involves a course of study leading to the award of a Certificate in Management Studies and guaranteed promotion.

Reversing decades of discrimination cannot, of course, be achieved overnight. There is still a long way to go. In the Fire Brigade, for instance, only 1 per cent of the 7,000 fire-fighters are from the ethnic minorities; more than half of these have been recruited since 1981. The number of female fire-fighters – a grand total of six – is too small to be expressed as a percentage.

What is certain is that the progress that has been made will be wiped out if the GLC is abolished. The government's opinion of the importance of the equal opportunities policy can be judged from the fact that none of the great tidal wave of documents gushing from Whitehall on the subject of the GLC has even mentioned the policy. This is in spite of the fact that the Commission for Racial Equality has told the government that 'the GLC equal opportunities policy is among the most developed of any authority.' Small wonder that organizations representing women and ethnic minorities have sounded the alarm:

> **The abolition of the GLC will probably affect ethnic minorities more than any other group in London.**
> National Council for Voluntary Organizations

> **The GLC must remain because we cannot afford to lose, and we believe London cannot afford to lose, a metropolitan authority that cares sufficiently about the injustices of a racist society to put race equality policies into practice.**
> Fight to Implement Race Equality, an umbrella organization representing 200 black and anti-racist groups

5 Safety first

> We've actually expanded the fire service
> because we weren't happy that Londoners' lives
> were not at risk unnecessarily when the last
> administration made cuts. And so there's no
> way the fire service isn't political. It is deeply
> political and Londoners' lives depend on it.
> *Ken Livingstone, GLC leader*, The London
> Programme, *4 November 1983*

On the evening of 21 January 1980 there was a fire at a
chemical warehouse in Barking. Two tonnes of sodium
chlorate exploded and clouds of dangerous gas were
released into the atmosphere. The GLC expert on the
spot had to advise on the evacuation of 6,000 residents
from the surrounding houses.

Later the same year, on 20 November 1980, propane
gas escaped from a glass factory in Harrow Weald. The
GLC scientific expert advised that 2,000 people should
be evacuated from the area.

'Expert' is precisely the word to use. Both these
people were members of the GLC's Scientific Services
Branch. It is internationally renowned for the knowledge
it has acquired over the years – knowledge which is now
threatened with dispersal by the government's plan to
abolish the GLC.

Scientists from the branch are on call 24 hours a day,
available to deal with many different types of emergency.
Greater London includes many factories using dangerous
chemicals, as well as pharmaceutical manufacturers,
hospitals and university departments dealing with radio-
active and bacteriological substances that are potentially

lethal. There is also an increasing number of lorries carrying hazardous loads on the capital's roads.

Since 1980 the Scientific Services Branch has had to attend 208 emergencies involving hazardous substances as well as giving advice on many others. In 44 of the emergencies people had to be evacuated.

One of the branch's most vital tasks is the expert advice and support it gives to London's fire-fighters. The London Fire Brigade is the largest in Europe, and the demands made on it are increasing all the time. In 1966, for instance, the brigade dealt with a total of 55,516 emergency calls. By 1981 this had risen to 107,807 and in 1983 – the busiest year in the brigade's history – there were no fewer than 117,000 calls answered. Nearly 1,000 people were rescued as a result.

☐ **To help fire-fighters at incidents involving chemicals and other hazardous substances the Fire Brigade has developed CIRUS (Chemical Information Retrieval and Updating System). Details of over 28,000 chemicals are stored on microfiche. The brigade also has a central risk register – a computerized system which catalogues thousands of addresses in the Greater London area and details of hazards, such as radiation, which may be stored there. This information can be passed within seconds to the scene of an incident.**

All this costs money, of course. On top of its running expenses, the brigade needs substantial capital investment. For example, the Fire Brigade's training centre at Southwark is a conglomeration of buildings, some temporary, some permanent, dating back to the eighteenth century in some cases. The centre might have been big enough to cope with the needs of a brigade covering the old London County Council area but it cannot deal properly with the expanding needs of a brigade covering the much larger GLC area and using modern equipment.

Although the total cost is likely to exceed £12 million the GLC is currently arranging to rebuild the training centre and the fire station nextdoor to it. The GLC can consider such a project, despite the government's restrictions on capital spending, because of its size and its ability to deploy funds across a wide range of services.

At the same time, the GLC has confirmed a programme of updating the fire stations themselves. The London Fire Brigade works from 114 stations built at various dates from 1983 onwards. Thirty-five of the earlier stations were designed for horse-drawn fire appliances. The current GLC policy is to build two new fire stations every year as well as refurbishing one major station. That means finding at least £3 million a year for capital spending.

A good deal of money is also spent in fire prevention. Advertising campaigns on television and hoardings remind people of the ways in which they can minimize fire risks. The Fire Brigade aims to visit every school in the GLC area at least once a year to talk to groups of pupils.

Meanwhile, the brigade's Fire Prevention Branch deals with buildings where fire prevention measures are required by law (such as offices, factories and hotels) and makes sure that the legal requirements are met and maintained. The branch also gives advice in connection with buildings which aren't controlled by fire precautions legislation but where fire safety is still desperately important – notably hospitals, schools, prisons and nursing homes. In an average year officers of the Fire Prevention Branch examine over 25,000 sets of building plans and carry out more than 50,000 inspections of premises.

☐ **One thing which the government can't abolish is the Thames Barrier at Woolwich Reach, which stands as a monument to British skill and ingenuity**

and to the GLC's efforts to protect London from flooding. It will serve the capital well until at least 2030. The government proposes to pass the barrier from the GLC into the hands of an unelected and unaccountable quango, the Thames Water Authority. Will the TWA take its responsibilities to Londoners as seriously as the GLC? It's anyone's guess. What is certain is that there is no way in which Londoners can put pressure on the authority if it doesn't do its duty.

Such services as fire prevention might seem uncontroversial enough. As Shirley Porter, Conservative leader of Westminster Council, exclaimed in exasperation during *The London Programme* in November 1983:

> If Ken Livingstone believes that the fire service is political then that's what's wrong with Ken Livingstone. I say it is not political. I say what you have to look at is the way it's run, and does it give value for money? That's got nothing to do with politics.

However, like it or not, decisions about money have a habit of being influenced by sordid old politics. And decisions about the money for London's Fire Brigade are no exception.

The government proposes that the Fire Brigade should be taken away from the GLC and given to a quango (yes, yet another one), the excitingly named London Fire and Civil Defence Authority. The authority will automatically be rate-capped for its first three years of existence. Indeed, Patrick Jenkin will be allowed to do pretty well whatever he likes with the authority. Clause 80 of the Abolition Bill empowers him to issue regulations 'with a view to securing that the functions of the new authority are discharged economically, efficiently and effectively.'

These 'regulations' enable the minister to intervene directly in the staffing, management, budget and policies of the new authority. And if the minister is still unhappy, Clause 40 of the Bill gives him the power to make an Order dismantling the London Fire and Civil Defence Authority. He can then group London boroughs together for the purpose of creating a number of Fire Boards scattered round London; or he can hand the function to individual boroughs, or to the counties surrounding London.

This last provision makes one wonder whether the government has given any thought to its proposals at all. It certainly indicates that the government has no great confidence in the authority that it intends to create. But the idea that individual boroughs could run their own fire brigades is clearly misconceived.

The government claims that the Fire and Civil Defence Authority will be 'democratic'. This is because each borough (and the City) will be allowed to nominate one councillor to sit on it.

This would hardly make it more democratic than the present system, even if the authority were to have any autonomy from the government. But the point is that the authority will be nothing but a puppet because of the powers which the Secretary of State will have over it. It is Patrick Jenkin and his colleagues who will decide how much can be spent on London's Fire Brigade, and the new authority – rate-capped from birth – will obey.

Judging by the past record of the government's assessment of how much needs to be spent on the Fire Brigade, one cannot feel much confidence for the future. Indeed, it seems highly likely that Londoners will die unnecessarily because of what the government wishes to do.

Every year the government produces a Grant Related Expenditure Assessment (GREA) which shows how much each council in Britain ought to spend on each service. In 1983–4 the government's estimate of how much needed to be spent on the London Fire Brigade was £19.6 million lower than the actual cost of the brigade for that year. In 1984–5 things went from bad to worse: the government's assessment of what the London Fire Brigade ought to spend was £20 million below the anticipated actual spending.

If the government really intends that the new authority will introduce an immediate cut of more than £20 million in the Fire Brigade's budget as soon as the GLC is abolished, it has a duty to show where these savings could come from. Needless to say, it has not done so.

All that has been said on the subject is studiously vague. At the end of October 1984, for instance, Leon Brittan, the Home Secretary, muttered threateningly that 'rigorous financial scrutiny' would have to be applied to all fire services and auditors would be asked to secure better 'value for money'. But even he did not suggest that £20 million would be saved from the London Fire Brigade simply by providing better 'value for money' (whatever that may mean in the context of fire brigades). The only way in which such a huge cut could be achieved would be by sacking hundreds of fire-fighters, closing fire stations and failing to maintain essential equipment.

To make matters worse, the new quango which takes over the London Fire Brigade will also inherit the GLC's responsibilities for civil defence. 'Civil defence' means protection for civilians against the effects of nuclear, chemical and conventional war, but the GLC – in common with 160 councils in Britain – has taken the view that there is no possible protection against nuclear war, and that it is futile to pretend otherwise. The Home Office's notorious pamphlet *Protect and Survive* claimed that people could shield themselves against nuclear weapons by whitewashing their houses or diving beneath the kitchen table. No expert agrees with this analysis.

Instead of encouraging people to whitewash their homes, the GLC has used its civil defence responsibility to alert Londoners to the facts about the nuclear threat. For example, it has opened London's nuclear bunkers to the public as well as staging exhibitions on the theme of

93

nuclear defence. And in 1984 it set up a Greater London Area War Risk Study to undertake detailed research into nuclear targets, weapons effects and the effectiveness of 'civil defence measures'.

However, if the GLC is abolished there is no doubt that the government and its new, Conservative-controlled Fire and Civil Defence Authority will immediately start spending money on civil defence programmes. But the authority's budget will be tightly controlled and rate-capped. So if the civil defence budget is to rise, then the amount spent on the fire service must fall.

In other words, the quango – with the government's blessing – will increase its spending on futile protection which would not save the lives of Londoners in a hypothetical nuclear war, at the expense of a service which actually does save the lives of Londoners every week of the year. Nothing could be more perfectly symbolic of the topsy-turvy sense of priorities which has characterized the government's attitude to abolition.

6 Fun and games

> The Metropolitan County Councils and the
> GLC have an excellent record on arts provision
> and I am delighted to pay wholly sincere
> tribute to it.
>
> *Lord Gowrie, Minister for the Arts*

London's cultural and sporting life is greatly influenced by the activities of local government. And local government in this case tends to mean the GLC.

There is nothing very surprising about that. Few people confine their leisure activities to the borough in which they happen to live. It is therefore natural that the job of supporting much of London's cultural, recreational and sporting life should fall to a city-wide authority such as the GLC. The council owns and runs 43 parks (including Battersea, Victoria, Dulwich, Holland, Crystal Palace and Hampstead Heath). It organizes 800 outdoor events every year ranging from small children's shows to spectacular annual occasions such as the Easter Parade, the Greater London Horse Show and Thamesday. It also provides the administrative support for the London Marathon. Many of these attract enormous support from the public. For example, the Thamesday held in September 1984 was attended by 300,000 people. And in October 1984 it was announced that more than 70,000 people had applied for places in the following year's London Marathon; unfortunately, there were only 17,000 places available. Even so, the London Marathon is still the biggest in the world.

> 66 **The day of mixed entertainment along the Embankment was well supported and there is no doubt that a large proportion of the public like and support this mixture of music, carnival atmosphere and water activity . . . It will be a pity if this overall type of free entertainment is denied Londoners, should the GLC be abolished. At times our city is not a very nice place to live and this kind of well-balanced free entertainment surely justifies the cost. 99**
>
> *The Stage*, September 1984, commenting on the fifth GLC Thamesday

Many people know that the GLC is heavily involved in the South Bank: it owns the concert halls (Royal Festival Hall, Queen Elizabeth Hall and Purcell Room) where its 'open foyer' policy has attracted hundreds of thousands of new visitors, and also subsidizes the other 'palaces of culture' – the National Theatre, National Film Theatre and Hayward Gallery.

What is less well known is that the GLC also gives financial support to hundreds of other groups in arts and entertainment. These range from major organizations, such as Sadlers Wells, to festivals, film and video companies, choirs and chamber groups, puppeteers, fringe theatres and many others.

Community arts and the arts of ethnic minorities in London have been notoriously underfunded in the past, but recently the GLC has gone some way towards remedying this. It has an annual budget of £1.5 million for community arts and another £1 million for ethnic minority arts.

Community arts projects supported include:

○ **North Paddington Community Darkroom** was granted £4,952 to help with darkroom facilities. It runs photography courses for local groups and helps to mount exhibitions and slide shows. It maintains a local picture library and takes photographs for community organizations.

○ **Age Exchange Theatre Company**, which was granted £31,150, works with pensioners, devising programmes around their reminiscences and their history. The group produces illustrated booklets of the research material supplied to it by pensioners.

○ **Tower Hamlets Senior Citizens' Film Association**, which was granted £10,681, provides films and videos for pensioners' clubs, day centres and hospitals. Pensioners choose the films, and discussions are organized to extend the educational potential of the scheme.

Examples of GLC-supported ethnic minority arts groups include:

○ **Carnival and Arts Committee**, the main organizer of the famous annual Notting Hill Carnival.

○ **Academy of Indian Dance**, with a grant of £19,348, was founded in 1979 with the aim of promoting Indian dance in Britain. It provides teaching to as high a standard as can be found in India.

○ **Theatro Technis** is a theatre group started by the Cypriot community in London 25 years ago. It also founded the Cypriot Advisory Service, helping Cypriots who have language problems or other difficulties.

Altogether, the GLC supports more than 400 arts and sports groups in London. It also owns and runs three historic houses from the eighteenth century – Kenwood, Marble Hill and Rangers House – and pays one-third of the running costs of the Museum of London.

As for physical recreation, it is hard to think of any sport with which the GLC is not involved in one way or another. It owns nearly 500 sports pitches, courts, tracks and baths. The GLC budget for sport in 1984–5 was £18 million. But not all its activities receive as much publicity as the London Marathon. For instance:

○ In September 1984 the GLC provided a grant to help an amateur **ice hockey** club in London from being disbanded.
○ In the same month a grant from the GLC made possible a test match at the Oval in **women's lacrosse** between the United States and England.
○ In November 1984 the GLC made an award of £36,480 to help reorganize **judo** coaching in several London boroughs.

The GLC runs 11 different sports championships in athletics, bowls, cross-country running, cycling (road and track), cyclo-cross, swimming, table tennis, golf, race-walking and orienteering. It provides coaching in tennis, football and athletics. Most notable of all, perhaps, it jointly funds the internationally famous Crystal Palace National Sports Centre.

All these different activities have a significant effect on the quality of life for Londoners. But a question mark now hangs over most of them as a result of the government's plans for abolishing the GLC. The arrangements made for them after abolition are a hopeless hotch-potch which could be disastrous for arts and recreation in London.

At the moment, all these cultural and sporting services are run by one body. After abolition, however, they will be thrown to the four winds.

The South Bank, for instance, will be passed to the Arts Council, which, as the Abolition Bill makes clear, will be kept under close ministerial scrutiny. The Arts Council, one need hardly point out, is an unelected and unaccountable quango (yes, *yet another* one). Just as importantly, it is entirely dependent on the government for its funds.

In recent years those funds have become increasingly scarce. In 1984 the Arts Council introduced a programme of massive cuts, killing off dozens of theatre groups and other bodies which depended on Arts Council grants. And that was before the Arts Council took on the additional responsibility of running the South Bank. If abolition does go through, it seems inevitable that the Arts Council will almost immediately be plunged into another financial crisis.

> 66 **The GLC and Metropolitan County Councils taken as a group have been the unquestioned leaders in the field of local authority support for the arts. From the council's point of view, it is difficult to envisage alternative arrangements which, taken as a whole, would serve the arts as well as those they are designed to replace.** 99
>
> Arts Council of Great Britain

While the Arts Council is to take over the South Bank and its 'palaces of culture', there is no mention in the government's proposals of what will happen to popular events that take place there. These include Thamesday (which attracts 300,000 people) and the South Bank Weekends (which have attracted up to 500,000). Presumably these and other events will simply be dropped.

Meanwhile, the hundreds of other groups in arts and recreation which are currently supported by the GLC will have to throw themselves on the tender mercies of the boroughs. Their chances of survival are slim. The Abolition Bill includes no safeguards for the future funding of community arts and ethnic minority arts by boroughs, nor for capital grants (that is, money for premises) which are given by the GLC at the moment.

On past form, it seems highly unlikely that many boroughs will maintain the GLC's level of support for these projects. In a paper outlining its 'proposals for the arts' the government said that it would expect borough councils 'to provide an appropriate level of support for arts activities'. It is not clear why the government should expect anything of the kind. Over the years, some London boroughs have shown no inclination at all to support the arts. Others have shown that the spirit is willing but the bank balance is weak. And now that the government has started its fiendish rate-capping exercise, the chances of individual councils setting aside money for the arts to fill the gap left by the GLC seem remote.

A good example of what is likely to happen to many groups if they have to rely on a borough for support is provided by the Riverside Studios in Hammersmith. This theatre and arts centre is internationally renowned, and attracts British and foreign performers of the highest calibre. However, two years ago Hammersmith Borough Council withdrew its funding and it seemed that the studios might have to close. The GLC stepped in with a grant of £400,000 which, for the Riverside Studios, was the difference between life and death.

If the GLC disappears, many other sporting or artistic ventures could find themselves in the same position – except that this time there will be no GLC to rescue them. No wonder the alarm has been sounded by organizations which are not usually to be found engaging in public controversy. In September 1984 a special conference organized by the Central Council for Physical Recreation passed a motion expressing concern at 'the most damaging consequences' to London's sport and re-creation which would be caused by abolition of the GLC.

This provoked an angry outburst from Neil Mac-Farlane, the Sports Minister, who said he was confident that local boroughs 'will have no difficulty in taking over the sport and recreation responsibilities of the GLC'. He did not explain how boroughs could do so if their budgets were being reduced. But he did add that, in any case, sports projects of 'wider than local significance' might be supported by . . . the Sports Council.

Yes, another quango.

7 A brighter city

Concerned as it is only with environmental quality, the trust can find nothing to commend in the White Paper proposals as they stand.
Civic Trust response to Streamlining the Cities

When Margaret Thatcher took her hasty decision to abolish the GLC, it seems unlikely that she gave much thought to its impact on the extraction of sand and gravel. Greater London consumes 10 million tonnes of the stuff every year, and the legacy of uncontrolled extraction in the past is more than 3,000 acres of derelict land in the capital. Indeed, it seems unlikely that Margaret Thatcher and her colleagues thought about any of the consequences for London's environment when they decided to abolish the GLC.

The River Thames has provided London with conveniently placed concentrations of sand and gravel which are an important source of raw materials for the construction industry. But the extraction of these minerals is understandably unpopular with local residents.

As the Minerals Planning Authority for London, the GLC tries to balance the need for the capital to provide some of its own requirements against the potential damage to the environment. The council employs four full-time specialists who carry out 400 site inspections a year to ensure that high standards of land restoration are achieved.

The council has established a system for handling planning applications from firms wanting to carry out mineral extraction. (It is responsible for all sites over five acres in central London.) Operators know that in dealing with a new application, the council will examine a company's previous record in handling similar sites.

The GLC has also co-operated with the Ministry of Agriculture in developing better methods of restoring land. It has started a £1 million programme to restore damaged land, which will try to tackle the mess left behind by uncontrolled operations before the council was set up.

Abolition will, of course, mean the complete disruption of this elaborate and carefully thought-out system. Devolution of mineral planning responsibilities to the boroughs involves breaking up the GLC's cost-effective team of specialists. Because the boroughs tend to take a local view of planning applications instead of looking at them in a London-wide context, more applications will be turned down: who would want mineral extraction to take place in *their* borough? This will result in increased building costs as firms have to import more raw materials from outside the capital.

At the same time, the unified standards now being applied across London will be threatened. The government's proposals could well result in a return to the lower standards of sand and gravel extraction which have left 3,000 acres of derelict land in the city. Nor can it be guaranteed that individual boroughs will give the same priority to the restoration of land which has already been damaged. And even if they do, where will they find the money to pay for it if they are already rate-capped?

This is far from being the only way in which London's environment is menaced by the government's plans. Patrick Jenkin's proposals for the Green Belt have been described as the gravest threat to the Green Belt's existence since it was established in the late 1930s. There are 88,800 acres of Green Belt in London, of which 12,800 acres are directly owned by the GLC. The council also owns 1,600 acres of Green Belt in land adjoining London, and has a part interest in another 27,000 acres.

The Green Belt is one of the great planning successes

of this century. It was set up to contain the sprawl of the city and to ensure that Londoners had access to undeveloped land. In spite of the popularity of the Green Belt policy, it has been under continual threat of development for both housing and commercial purposes.

As planning authority for the area, the GLC advises other councils on any planning applications which will affect the Green Belt. It considers 800 or so applications every year and recommends refusal in about 85 per cent of cases. It gives the go-ahead only for small developments which do not affect the open character of the land; an application to build a D-I-Y superstore is unlikely to find favour.

As well as protecting Green Belt land from unsuitable development, the GLC has also taken a number of initiatives to improve that land. They include:

○ Landscape improvements to farm holdings, including a tree-planting programme costing £80,000 a year.
○ Educational access to the countryside. The Park Lodge Farm Centre is visited by thousands of people, and hundreds of school visits are made to the council's farms. In 1983 the Park Lodge Farm won a special Conservation Award.
○ The creation of country parks – Trent Park, Warren House Estate and Hainault. More than 1,800 acres have been or will be devoted to five country parks with easy access from Inner London boroughs which lack open space.
○ Collaboration with other public authorities to restore the landscape and create parks on land broadly in private ownership – the Lea, Colne and Roding Valleys, and in the Dagenham corridor.
○ Supporting Countryside Management Projects in areas where land is in multiple ownership, to reduce the conflict between the needs for recreation and agriculture.
○ Designating the Green Chain of open space in

south-east London and carrying out improvements in the landscape.

As a strategic authority, the GLC looks at the Green Belt as a whole when considering applications for development. It takes into account the needs of people in Islington, for instance, when it receives an application affecting Crayford Marshes.

Patrick Jenkin now proposes to transfer ownership of the GLC's Green Belt land to the relevant borough or county council in whose area it falls. These councils would be free to do as they wish with their newly acquired land – even to sell it if they could persuade the Secretary of State that they needed the money. (Which some of them certainly will after rate-capping.)

Land which is partly owned by the GLC will also pass into the ownership of the council which co-owns it at the moment. It is easy to demonstrate what effect this could have. In 1981 Berkshire County Council asked the GLC to agree to the sale of the greater part of the 128-acre Ankerwycke Estate at Wraysbury. Ankerwycke Farm, next to Magna Carta Island at Runnymede, was originally bought by Buckinghamshire County Council with a 40 per cent contribution from the old London County Council and Middlesex County Council. After the reorganization of local government, the farm passed to the Royal County of Berkshire.

The GLC opposed the sale of the farm, which lies within the Colne Valley Regional Park. As a result, Berkshire did not go ahead with the sale. But there is no guarantee that Berkshire will stick to this decision when the land passes entirely into its control. If the Secretary of State did consent to such a sale in the future, he or she could at the same time free the land from its current restrictive covenants, thereby placing a historic piece of land at grave risk of development.

Another example of the attitude of some public authorities to Green Belt land occurred in 1982, when Essex County Council asked the GLC to agree to the sale of 1,600 acres of Green Belt land which it had bought with financial aid from the old LCC. Most of the land consisted of farm holdings on the fringe of north-east London. Several would be split by the M25 motorway, and the GLC was concerned that private developers would not restore the land on either side of the motorway corridor to the high standard considered desirable by the council.

After the GLC expressed its opposition to the plan, Essex didn't pursue its intention to sell. But the GLC believes the county council is simply biding its time until abolition.

What happens to Green Belt land after the GLC loses control can be illustrated by the case of Gildenhall Farm at Swanley in Kent. In 1981 the GLC granted a lease on the 299-acre farm to a tenant farmer. As the farm is well away from the metropolitan area, the council believed it would be safe from development. Far from it; the tenant granted a 998-year lease to a second farmer, who immediately removed all hedges, ponds and trees, ploughed up footpaths and bulldozed parts of the land. This he did in order to cultivate cereal crops more efficiently. The result is, of course, that the farm has been completely devastated.

Although Patrick Jenkin justifies his plan for removing the Green Belt from the control of any strategic planning authority by saying that he regards Green Belt land as inalienable, past experience suggests otherwise. In 1981 the GLC was informed that the London Borough of Hillingdon wanted to develop 5.8 acres of land, known as Clarke's Meadows, for housing. The GLC asked the Secretary of State to intervene in this clear contravention of Green Belt policy, but he chose not to do so. If the GLC is abolished, the same will probably happen elsewhere in the Green Belt.

66 The government proposals are shallow and inadequate and fail to find a way to best serve the interests of Londoners. Under the plans, the people in greatest need of the Green Belt – the

**three million residents of Inner London –
would have no say. 99**

George Nicholson, Chair of GLC
Planning Committee

The Green Belt is often referred to as 'the lungs of
London', a description that is also applied to the 5,500
acres of parks and other open spaces owned by the GLC.
They include Hampstead Heath, Battersea Park, Victoria
Park, Crystal Palace Park and Holland Park. The GLC is
also developing new ones, such as Burgess and Mile End
Parks.

The government's plan is simple: hand the parks
over to the boroughs. It is also unworkable.

Important metropolitan parks and open space often
span more than one borough – Hampstead Heath and
Blackheath, for instance. How would two or three
different boroughs divide the responsibilities for manag-
ing a park which fell within the borders of all of them?

Moreover, the *users* of GLC parks come from more
than one borough. Hampstead Heath, for example, attracts
visitors from all over London – for walking, sunbathing,
frisbee-throwing, kite-flying or simply staring at the
scenery. Parks such as that are an asset to all Londoners.
Why should the burden of upkeep be dumped on just one
or two boroughs? As the GLC Conservative Group put it
in their response to the government:

Boroughs may not be keen to pay for the
upkeep of parks of regional significance.

The point was echoed by the Civic Trust, which doubted

whether individual boroughs and districts have
the will, resources or the landscape expertise
to assume responsibility for the maintenance
of country parks, the larger parks in London,
and the creation of new ones, particularly in
circumstances when many of the users will not
be ratepayers in the area.

There is certainly little prospect of Southwark and Tower Hamlets – two of the most deprived areas in London – having the resources to complete the development of Burgess and Mile End Parks.

The more one studies the government's plan, the more one realizes that it is not a plan at all. The government simply cannot have given any thought to the consequences of its action; for a moment's thought would show (for example) that parks cannot be handed over lock, stock and barrel to the boroughs.

The same is true of the government's proposal for another matter which is crucial to London's environment – waste disposal. If the government had thought its proposals out carefully, one would have expected it to consult experts in the field. It did not. But here is what the experts have to say. The Institute of Wastes Management:

> Unless waste disposal is operated over reasonably large areas there can be no economy of scale, no rationalization of facilities, no effective long-term strategic planning ... There is no informed impartial opinion known to the institute and its members that is other than complimentary about improvements in the control and disposal of waste since this function became the responsibility, in London, of the GLC.

And the National Association of Waste Disposal Contractors, which represents the private sector:

> This association ... does not believe that any benefit can be gained by passing the responsibilities of the GLC and Metropolitan Counties to the London boroughs and Metropolitan District Councils.

As with so many of the arrangements for taking over GLC services, Whitehall hasn't done its homework.

The GLC gets rid of 3.25 million tonnes of household waste every year in up-to-date transfer stations. It is a huge task. Every week most Greater London households throw out more than 40 pounds of rubbish – 14 per cent of all the rubbish Britain chucks away.

Modern refuse disposal demands technology at a level which individual boroughs cannot afford. Thanks to its size, the GLC has also been able to afford research into its own new technology. It now leads Europe in the production of electricity from waste. Rubbish burned at the Edmonton incinerator produces £3.7 million-worth of electricity a year and the GLC has successfully reclaimed methane gas from a rubbish tip at Aveley which is then piped to nearby factories.

The GLC has also led the country in bottle-bank schemes and recycling centres, recovering thousands of tonnes of glass and metal, and tens of thousands of gallons of oil.

Even the government has been forced to concede that it would be impossible for individual boroughs working on their own to take over the job of waste disposal. *Streamlining the Cities* explained:

> In most cases it is the government's view that authorities will need to make co-operative arrangements for the discharge of these functions over the whole, or, in the case of London, large sections of, the metropolitan area.

How might these 'co-operative arrangements' work? The Abolition Bill itself is utterly vague on the point. It says merely that the Secretary of State will have the power, where he considers that groups of boroughs 'could with advantage make joint arrangements' and 'have not made any satisfactory arrangement for that purpose', to establish a 'single authority' by order. None of these terms is defined in the Bill, so we don't know what this 'authority' might look like. All we know is that the government thinks that waste disposal can be taken over by some kind of 'joint committees' of boroughs, but that if that fails the government itself will step in.

As with quite a few of the abolition proposals, there is a strong sense of *déjà vu* about all this. For the 'voluntary co-operative arrangements' on which the government is pinning its hopes have already been tried. In 1947, after long disagreement between London's local authorities, boroughs were put together in groups for the purpose of waste disposal. These were 'voluntary groupings' like the ones the government is suggesting now. But they didn't work, because the boroughs found it impossible to co-operate with one another. By the time the Herbert Commission reported 13 years later, in 1960, eight of the ten groupings had already disbanded in disarray. As Herbert commented:

> The whole system is, in our opinion,
> unhealthy from the point of view of good local
> government, unbusinesslike and wasteful in
> land use.

As a result of this failure, waste disposal was given to the GLC when it was formed in 1964. As the GLC Conservative Group has recently pointed out:

> The economies of scale resulting from the
> institution of a London-wide, unified service
> have resulted in far greater efficiency. The
> system has, in short, already been streamlined.
> Since 1963, three rail systems have been
> closed, nine road stations, seven river stations,
> 16 incinerators, one composting plant and one
> pulverizing plant – i.e. 74 per cent of the plants
> inherited.

Yet the government is now apparently determined to put the clock back 20 years or more, and to force London's waste disposal service to return to the chaos of the 1950s. The leading professional body in the field, the Institute of Wastes Management, is unequivocal in its attitude: the government's plans are a load of rubbish.

The suggested solution of voluntary co-operation by district or borough authorities in some form or other . . . ignores the reality of the situation. All experiences in the past in this field indicate quite firmly that voluntary co-operation between three or four boroughs has in the end failed completely, let alone between a much greater number of authorities as envisaged in the consultation document. Members of this institute consider it naive to think that authorities of widely different political outlook will work together. They have not done so in the past and it is even more unlikely now.

8 A little learning

I am unemployed at the moment and find that both the day and evening classes I attend not only fill in time that would otherwise be wasted but have also given me practical experience to maybe enable me to seek work in other fields in the future. Surely the education of people is a sign of a civilized country? Without help from the Inner London Education Authority, the cost of further education would be beyond the range of most people, especially the ones that need it most.

Letter sent to ILEA in 1984

It would be unfair to say that the present government never sees the error of its ways. Under the original plans for abolishing the GLC, education in Inner London was to be put in the hands of a new joint board of councillors. The present Inner London Education Authority, a special committee of the GLC, was to be abolished.

The reaction to this plan was, to put it mildly, unfriendly. Sir Keith Joseph, the Education Secretary, received 2,003 letters on the issue; all but three of them opposed his plans.

The government announced that it had had a change of heart. After abolition of the GLC, education in Inner London would be run by a directly elected Inner London Education Authority. Democracy had triumphed, it seemed.

However, one swallow doesn't make a summer, and one concession definitely doesn't make a U-turn. Apart from changing its mind over the quango, the government is as determined as ever to devastate London's education system. And it should be remembered that 'education' in this context means not only primary and secondary schools but also further education, polytechnics, adult education, evening classes and so on.

Nor is it actually certain that a directly elected ILEA will survive after all. The government's Abolition Bill gives ministers astonishing powers – including the power to change their minds yet again. Clause 21 of the Bill allows a Secretary of State (not even the Education Secretary) to abolish the Inner London Education Authority *at any time*. Moreover, if Patrick Jenkin wishes to destroy or limit the powers of ILEA, he can give some or all of the authority's functions to the boroughs. He could thus hive off adult education, for example, or primary schools, to the boroughs or to a new educational quango on which boroughs are represented.

In other words, despite having promised to 'save' ILEA, the government has left itself the chance of killing it off at any time after abolishing the GLC. Under the Bill, ILEA could be abolished by an Order which would be subject to parliament's 'affirmative procedure': only one and a half hours of debate would take place in the Commons and no amendments to the Order would be debatable.

Even if Patrick Jenkin does not go so far as to abolish ILEA, he will still have a tight grip round its throat. Clause 80 of the Abolition Bill empowers him to issue regulations 'with a view to securing that the functions of the new authority are discharged economically, efficiently and effectively' for a period of three years up to April 1989.

The staffing, budget, management and policies of the new ILEA will thus be dictated by a Secretary of State, even if the appearance of democracy will be preserved by having elected members on the authority.

One can gain a pretty good idea of how the government will force ILEA to behave by looking at its past statements. Ministers have consistently claimed that the present ILEA is wildly extravagant. At the end of

1984 the government proposed a rate tantamount to a cut of £101 million in ILEA's budget.

The government's reason for thinking ILEA extravagant is apparently that ILEA spends more than other local education authorities. But this is hardly surprising. ILEA is the biggest education authority in Britain, with 296,787 children in its schools and another 454,890 students in further, higher and adult education. Moreover, on any known indicator ILEA emerges as an authority with exceptional – indeed unique – needs:

- 16 per cent of pupils in ILEA schools speak a language other than English at home; in all, 147 languages are spoken by ILEA schoolchildren.
- There are 30 per cent more handicapped children in London than nationally.
- 40 per cent of children in ILEA schools are eligible for free school meals.
- A quarter of children in ILEA schools come from broken homes.
- Unemployment in much of the inner city is around 18 per cent, and among the 16–19 age group the figures are much higher.
- ILEA provides 25 per cent of all adult education in the country.
- Half of ILEA's secondary school buildings and a quarter of its primary schools were built before the turn of the century. A 1984 report showed that ILEA should be spending about £30 million a year just on replacing old buildings to a modern standard. For 1984–5 ILEA's actual bid was for £26 million; but the Department of Education and Science decided to allocate only £9.7 million.
- To fulfil targets set in 1973 by Margaret Thatcher, when she was Education Secretary, for rebuilding or remodelling primary schools built in the nineteenth century, ILEA would need about £115 million. At the moment, most

pre-1900 buildings will not be improved until after the year 2000.

It is also worth pointing out that the difference between ILEA's budget and those of other education authorities may not be caused by ILEA's 'extravagance' so much as by other authorities' underspending. Her Majesty's Inspectorate of Schools has advised parliament that of 96 English local education authorities, only six are adequately resourced: one of those is ILEA.

The government's belief that ILEA is over-lavish is not shared by Londoners – even by the government's own supporters. According to a MORI opinion poll published in October 1984:

- 78 per cent of Inner Londoners oppose the government's plan to cut ILEA's spending by £75 million.
- 51 per cent of Conservatives are opposed.
- Only 7 per cent of Inner Londoners – and only 22 per cent of Conservatives – are in favour of the cut.
- 82 per cent of Inner Londoners favour either increasing education spending and rates or keeping spending and rates at their present levels.
- Even among Conservative supporters, 54 per cent favour keeping rates and spending at current levels and 21 per cent would like to see an increase in both spending and rates.

In fact, it is not ILEA's spending which is unreasonable but the government's behaviour. ILEA receives no block grant at all and has not done so since 1980–1. If it received grant aid at the national average rate it would have had funding to the tune of £350 million in 1984–5 – which would pay for more than a third of its spending of £923 million. Instead, ILEA has to raise the whole sum through the rates. Thanks to the irrational way in which the government calculates Grant Related Expenditure (which in turn determines how much grant an authority should get), ILEA's ratepayers are forced to shoulder the burden.

To have received any grant at all in 1984–5 ILEA would have had to reduce its total spending to less than £638 million – a cut of 31 per cent in its budget. As the *Municipal Journal* remarked in September 1984:

> The equity of the system seems questionable when one considers that in real terms ILEA's estimated expenditure before income will be about 3.3 per cent lower in 1984–5 than it was in 1978–9. Over the same time scale manpower [*sic*] levels have dropped by 1,000.

To make the system even less equitable the government then announced its demand for a further £75 million cut in ILEA spending as part of its rate-capping programme. ILEA officials calculated that these cuts would involve

- A £4 million cut in the programme of removing asbestos from schools – a cut which would put children's health at risk
- A 43 per cent increase in school meal prices
- A 30 per cent reduction in school allowances
- Deterioration in staffing ratios to cut over 700 teaching posts in schools
- Ending the school clothing voucher scheme which currently benefits 55,460 pupils
- Leaving new nursery classes unopened
- Ending the provision of free school milk
- A 30 per cent cut in discretionary student awards
- The closure of youth clubs and sports centres
- Substantial cuts in adult education

There would also be massive cuts in building maintenance and support services. More than 5,000 full-time jobs would be lost. Since many of ILEA's employees are part-time, the actual number affected would be far greater.

ILEA refused to make these cuts. Such defiance is difficult enough at the moment, because of the number of powers that the government has acquired over local government in recent years. But it would be impossible if the GLC were abolished and a 'new' ILEA came into existence, its every move dictated and controlled by the Secretary of State. If the new ILEA continued to show any signs of defiance, the Secretary of State could simply abolish it.

Fears that this might happen were hardly set at rest by Sir Keith Joseph's performance during the Second Reading debate on the Abolition Bill in December 1984. He made a revealing slip:

> I was in at the birth of the GLC . . . I am assisting at the obsequies of ILEA.
> [*Interruption*] I was in at the birth of the GLC and now I am assisting at its obsequies – perhaps that is better.

9 Who pays?

> At least the GLC's statistics are tangible, itemized and debatable. The government gives the impression of having conjured figures out of the air to justify a policy hastily cobbled together.
>
> Guardian, *23 November 1984*

London encompasses extremes of wealth and poverty. It includes the poorest borough in Britain (Hackney) and the richest (the City). The existence of the GLC helps to reduce the inequalities by transferring money from richer areas to poorer ones. To take just one example, that of the concessionary fares scheme: Westminster pays £8.37 million into the scheme but receives £1.72 million, while Lewisham contributes £0.91 million but receives £1.92 million.

The government promises that this intricate system of redistribution will survive if the GLC is abolished. It has promised to extend the London Rate Equalization Scheme to this end: the spirit of Robin Hood will live on.

We shall see. But there are grounds for doubting the government's assurance. A detailed study – the only detailed study, since the government hasn't bothered to do any – was commissioned by the GLC to estimate what would have happened to borough rates if the GLC had already been abolished in 1984 and its services were carried on at the same level. The results were striking:

○ Ratepayers in inner-city boroughs, such as Islington, Hackney, Tower Hamlets and Hammersmith and Fulham, would be worst affected. The largest increase in rates would be 17.6p in Islington – almost a 40 per cent increase in the rate charged for GLC services.

○ Ratepayers in many other London boroughs – mainly under Conservative control – would face rises too. Conservative-controlled Outer London boroughs would have rate rises of between 1.5p (Waltham Forest) and 6.8p (Merton).

○ Outer London boroughs with inner-city problems would fare particularly badly. Haringey's rate poundage would rise by 11.1p and Newham's by 8.3p. In fact, all London's authorities which are on the government's list of the top twenty 'most deprived' council areas would suffer rate increases.

○ The two authorities which would benefit most from abolition would be those which are already by far the richest in rateable values. The end of the GLC would cut Westminster's rate poundage by 5.1p and the City of London's by 7p – even after taking into account their contributions to the extended Rate Equalization Scheme.

❝❝Once the London Rate Equalization Scheme has been extended to redistribute a very large amount of money, that is bound to hand to the Secretary of State in Marsham Street considerable control over how much is collected from the wealthy boroughs and how much redistributed to the rest. And inevitably he will personally be responsible for deciding what the rate bills are in the end in both those wealthy central London boroughs and throughout the rest of London.

And that must mean a considerable transfer of control from town hall to Whitehall. 🙿

Tony Travers, Research Fellow in Local Government, *The London Programme*, 4 November 1983

One example of the way in which GLC abolition would make the rich boroughs richer at the expense of the rest comes from the arrangements for funding voluntary organizations if the GLC goes. Under the Abolition Bill, borough councils will be empowered to make grants to London-wide organizations. If a borough has previously won the agreement of two-thirds of all London boroughs to the grant, it can recover a proportion of the grant and administrative costs from all boroughs. But there's a catch. Costs will be divided between the boroughs on the basis of their population.

This extraordinary innovation of dividing costs according to a borough's population rather than its rateable value will end the redistribution currently achieved by the GLC precept. The City's contribution would fall from 17.8 per cent to 0.08 per cent, because hardly anyone lives in the City. However, the City is immensely wealthy because of the huge rateable value of its office buildings. Why shouldn't it put some of its surplus cash to the service of less fortunate Londoners?

More to the point, perhaps, is the question of who will fill the gap left by the City and the other rich boroughs. The less well-off boroughs clearly cannot be expected to take on the whole burden themselves. So what will happen is that voluntary organizations will have their grants cut, or stopped altogether.

The supposedly 'controversial' grants would certainly be the first for the chop. Some boroughs have made it clear that they would not be prepared to fund these even if the money was available. The grants in question are those to groups concerned with women, ethnic minorities and gay people.

The GLC has put out some publications pointing out that it funds well over 2,000 voluntary organizations of which less than 1.5 per cent might be considered remotely controversial. But why is there any need to be defensive on the subject? For example, there are probably more than half a million lesbians and gay men in London. They pay rates just like anyone else. Why shouldn't the council support them?

Similarly, a great fuss from the tabloid press can be guaranteed whenever the GLC gives a grant to a women's project. Yet these same tabloid papers never dream of objecting to the fact that, for instance, the GLC pays for dozens of football pitches which are almost exclusively of benefit to men and boys.

But this is not an argument which finds favour with all London's borough councils. However defensible the GLC's grants may be, there is no doubt that many – probably most – of them will not continue after abolition.

> ❝ The loss of GLC funding, unless accompanied by a dramatic increase in funding from the boroughs, would inevitably result in a cut-back in the vital services we provide to this disadvantaged group of children. ❞
>
> National Association of Deaf, Blind and Rubella Handicapped

The GLC's grants to certain organizations have sometimes been used by ministers as examples of the council's 'profligacy', and as evidence in favour of abolishing it. The Prime Minister has described the GLC as an 'enormous drain on the ratepayer' and this theme has been eagerly taken up by her colleagues.

The first point that needs to be made is that the government should remember the old line about people in glass houses not throwing stones. The GLC's increases in spending between 1978 and 1983 came to a total of 88 per cent. This was lower than the rates of increase in the

Average Earnings Index and the Retail Price Index over the same period. More significantly, it was considerably lower than the increase in spending by *central* government, which came to 101 per cent.

Then there is the question of the rates. Margaret Thatcher is quite right to say that the GLC's rates have risen sharply, as have those of some London borough councils. This has happened for a perfectly simple reason: the government has been allocating less from national taxation to local government. So a greater proportion of councils' spending has to come from locally raised revenue – in other words, the rates.

Between 1979–80 and 1983–4, cuts in the government's Rate Support Grant took away more than £1,700 million from London – an average of about £370 from every household paying rates, not to mention commercial and industrial ratepayers. In other words, rates have gone to subsidize central government spending. As no less an authority than the *Financial Times* put it, in an editorial in December 1983:

> The government cuts have taken £3.6 billion
> of grant away from councils since 1978–9,
> nearly half of it from London. The total grant
> loss is the equivalent of 4p in the pound on
> income tax and the government is less than
> just in not admitting that this switch in tax
> burden from central to local is at least partly
> responsible for rate rises.

Thus the government's arguments on both the cost and the rate level of the present GLC are wrong. And the cost of abolishing the GLC will be met by those least able to afford it: voluntary groups and others who have had their grants taken away; ex-GLC employees made redundant; borough councils already reeling from rate-capping.

One point that is now beyond doubt is that the plethora of arrangements to replace the GLC will cost more than the present council. The government has persistently claimed that there will be 'substantial' savings from abolition but until the end of 1984 it had always refused to be more specific. Then, in November 1984, it announced that the abolition of the GLC would save £50 million.

This was the figure that was described by the *Guardian* as having been conjured out of the air. The government was quite unable to say where the figure had come from or to produce the calculations on which it was based. The GLC, on the other hand, had by then come up with an itemized account which suggested that abolition would not save Londoners a penny; indeed, it would cost them £225 million.

This confirmed the conclusions of every expert study into the matter. Coopers and Lybrand predicted that 'there could be significant extra costs.' PA Management Consultants found that

> The problems of transition are substantial, and are likely to involve considerable costs. There appear to be so few long-term benefits arising from the proposed reorganization that the immediate costs of transition . . . are unlikely to be offset by longer-term gains in efficiency and effectiveness.

Yet Patrick Jenkin has continued, ever since May 1983, to rabbit on about the 'significant savings to arise from the abolition of the GLC'. During the Paving Bill debates in May 1984 this all became too much for one Tory MP, Sir Kenneth Lewis, who commented:

> The minister will spell out what he will save on this. He should halve the figure and if he waits for a few more years he will lose even that half. I do not think that in the end we shall save anything.

10 The future

> It is in local hands that local control belongs.
> It is into local hands that local control should
> be put ... We have measured the GLC for its
> concrete overshoes and in 1986 over the
> parapet and into the Thames it goes.
> *Lord Bellwin, Local Government Minister,*
> *Conservative Party Conference, October 1983*

The GLC is not perfect. No political institution is. But it
has served Londoners reasonably well for 20 years, as its
predecessor, the LCC, did for 75 years before that. It is
also the regional government of the capital city of Great
Britain. As such, it deserves rather more respect than
ministers have shown it. Lord Bellwin's gleefully dismissive remarks about shoving the GLC over the parapet in
its concrete overshoes are typical of the juvenile,
raspberry-blowing attitude which has characterized the
approach of many – though not all – of the GLC's critics.

Perhaps the government is forced to rely on crude
abuse because it is incapable of defending its proposals
for the GLC in a calm, rational argument. The proposals
have been condemned by almost every expert body
which has had any dealings with the GLC, including
many which are politically opposed to the present
administration at County Hall. Over the months it has
become clearer and clearer that no thought at all was
given to the abolition proposal before it was inserted in
the Conservative manifesto.

All previous reorganizations of local government
have been preceded by a proper inquiry – perhaps even a
royal commission. Nothing of the sort has happened this

time. There wasn't even a parliamentary debate on the White Paper *Streamlining the Cities*. The government has also refused to appoint any experts – accountants, consultants and so on – to see how its proposals might work. Presumably this is because the government is afraid of getting the answer that it doesn't want to hear: that it should drop its plans altogether.

Of course, it is possible that a full inquiry into the GLC, considering all the possibilities, might come up with some suggestions for reform (although the last inquiry, that led by Sir Frank Marshall in 1977, found that the GLC was in pretty good shape). There is nothing sacrosanct about the present structure. Indeed, in the past few months several proposals for reform rather than abolition have been put forward.

The trouble with these proposals, however, is that they are back to front. They assume that the government will abolish the GLC unless someone can produce a scheme that will avoid abolition but will allow the government to save face. They are thus attempts to salvage something from the wreckage rather than reflections on the GLC's present performance and ways in which it can be improved:

○ Some MPs have suggested a Grand Committee of the 84 London MPs, which would be nothing more than a talking shop. As the *Economist* has commented: 'It would have no powers. And no point.'

○ Others have proposed making the London Boroughs' Association a statutory 'forum' for London. This is another non-starter: the LBA represents only Tory councils. Labour boroughs are in the Association of London Authorities.

○ The GLC Conservative Group has proposed a new London-wide body 'with its specific functions precisely conferred on it by legislation.' It would only be allowed to discharge these functions and the Secretary of

State would retain reserve powers to direct its work.

○ The SDP–Liberal Alliance favours incorporating the GLC into a new form of government with regional responsibilities for an area far beyond the confines of the present GLC. The drawback to this scheme is that there must be some point at which the GLC's borders stop spreading. The council already represents seven million people. If a halt is not called somewhere the GLC will end up running the whole of Britain.

Although these ideas have their flaws, there would be nothing to prevent a thorough inquiry considering them in greater detail, and at greater leisure, along with many other ideas. But the government has no time for thinking. It apparently feels that the world will end if the GLC isn't abolished by April 1986.

In these circumstances, there is little one can do but accept that the GLC's present structure works pretty well. There is no point, at the moment, in looking for minor improvements, for the government isn't interested in them. The immediate task is to save the GLC.

It may seem hopeless, given the size of the government's majority in the House of Commons, but there are grounds for mild optimism. The government has already suffered several setbacks. Its attempt to change the political control of the council in 1985 without elections was thwarted. It had to back down from its insistence on replacing ILEA with a quango.

The government has also found itself in the embarrassing position of being attacked just as vigorously by its own backbenchers as by the opposition. The Abolition Bill will be fought every inch of the way. At the same time expert groups will be telling the government over and over again that its proposals are unworkable. And many civil servants are known to be deeply worried by the impossibility of putting the government's plans into practice.

Under such pressure, would the government carry on regardless? Perhaps. But there is at least a chance that it may at last heed the advice given to the House of Commons by an MP in February 1975:

> We should resist the imposition of new taxes and new systems of government.

The speaker was Kenneth Baker, the man who now has the job of imposing a new, chaotic and unwanted system of government on the people of London.

Index